From My Heart to Yours

Hundreds of Prayers for All Your Cares

NANCY ROBERTS

WESTBOW®
PRESS
A DIVISION OF THOMAS NELSON
& ZONDERVAN

All Scriptures taken from *The Holy Bible, New International Version*. Copyright 1973, 1978, 1984 by International Bible Society.

WestBow Press books may be ordered through booksellers or by contacting:

WestBow Press
A Division of Thomas Nelson & Zondervan
1663 Liberty Drive
Bloomington, IN 47403
www.westbowpress.com
1 (866) 928-1240

ISBN: 978-1-4908-4122-9 (sc)
ISBN: 978-1-4908-4121-2 (hc)
ISBN: 978-1-4908-4123-6 (e)

Library of Congress Control Number: 2014910891

Printed in the United States of America.

WestBow Press rev. date: 7/15/2014

Pray continually.

—1 Thessalonians 5:17

Did you know the words *heart* and *hearts* appear in the Bible (New International Version) over seven hundred times? Neither did I until they started coming up repeatedly in my personal devotion time. I decided the Lord was trying to tell me something, so I prayed about it.

I have kept a journal for years because praying and writing have always gone hand in hand for me. Many of these prayers are personal; some have to do with what is going on in the world; and others are just conversations with God. He and I have grown closer through our quiet, daily prayer time. The Lord also has given me the opportunity to pray with friends and family over the phone, through e-mail, and in person. God is available anytime, anywhere. He loves to hear from his children. I am a prayer warrior: this is a battle I cannot fight alone. Join me in conversations with our heavenly Father, Jesus, the Holy Spirit, Abba, and Lord, our dearest friend. Let's pray for and with each other, too. The eloquence of the words we say is not important; it's what's in our hearts that matters. So join me in a word of prayer today. Our friend is waiting to hear from us.

Psalm 116:6

The Lord protects the simple-hearted; when I was in great need he saved me.

Lord, what does it mean to be simple-hearted? Does it mean simpleminded? I don't think so. Maybe it means I can only handle so much. I'd have to ask you for help then, wouldn't I? Lord, pride gets in the way sometimes. I need a Savior. I need you. Please take the anxiousness from my heart and replace it with trust. I need you like I need air, water, food, and shelter. I'll keep this simple: you're my Savior, and I need you.

Amen.

Proverbs 22:17–19

Pay attention and listen to the sayings of the wise; apply your heart to what I teach, for it is pleasing when you keep them in your heart and have them ready on your lips. So that your trust may be in the Lord, I teach you today, even you.

"The enemy of good is better." My coworker told me that today, and it stuck with me. Lord, there's a lot of truth in this statement; when someone like me, a perfectionist from the get-go, hears it, I definitely take it to heart. Lord, wisdom isn't something you get overnight or buy at a store. No, quite to the contrary—it is earned. Earned through (actually, if you put an *"L"* in front of *earned*, you get *learned*) much perseverance and perhaps making a few mistakes along the way. Help me, Lord, to apply what I've learned to new situations. Keep my brain fresh and receptive to new ideas. May my wisdom never grow stale, for you created me with a mind that (without sounding conceited) is a miracle. We're *all* miracles. I trust in your creation, and I trust in you, Lord. Help my brain to never forget that fact.

Amen.

Psalm 13:5–6

I will trust in your unfailing love; my heart rejoices in your salvation. I will sing to the Lord, for he has been good to me.

Lord, I like to sing. I don't have a voice that's Broadway-worthy, but I do love music. Music is a timeline for me: it marks time's passage in my life far too swiftly. Nevertheless, time is nothing to you, Lord—the blink of an eye and a millennium are both the same to you. I will sing with the choir of saints in heaven someday, but until then my heart rejoices in your goodness to me.

Amen.

Psalm 86:12

I will praise you, O Lord my God, with all my heart; I will glorify your name forever.

Oh Jesus, I do not feel much like praising you today. My voice would quiver and crack, and I couldn't sing any upbeat song. (Well, frankly, I couldn't on a good day. I'm not much of a singer.) However, I can write.

If you wallow in your sorrow, there's nothing good tomorrow.

If you pray, in *your today*; the Lord will have his say.

So tonight, turn out the light, knowing it will be all right.

I'll glorify your holy name forever.

There's my silly little poem. I offer it with all my heart, even though I'm feeling blue. I feel better knowing you listen to me, and for that reason I will glorify your holy name forever.

Amen.

Ephesians 1:18

I pray also that the eyes of your heart may be enlightened in order that your may know the hope to which he called you, the riches of his glorious inheritance in the saints.

Open the eyes of my heart, Lord; I do want to see you. I know that all those wonderful folks who have gone before us into your glorious heaven are looking down upon us here on earth, and they're singing your praises and just basking in your glorious presence, Lord. This will be my inheritance someday, but for now, I have a job to do here, don't I? Clear my vision to your ways, so that I may see and do what you require of me here today.

Amen.

Psalm 73:26

My flesh and my heart may fail, but God is the strength of my heart and my portion forever.

Father, strength to me means muscle—lots of muscles. Strength, however, envelops more than that. Being strong sometimes means being patient while you wait on God's timing—right, Lord? Strength comes from enduring trials, too. Strength can mean holding on to what's right but letting go of past mistakes and failures. Having strength can mean struggling through or perhaps taking the high road when it's not the easiest road to take. Father, I pray for strength today, to make it through, to be led by you, or perhaps carried. Give me the strength to back off if necessary, so others can be strong in you, too. Help my heart to be strong all day long.

Amen.

Romans 5:5

And hope does not disappoint us, because God has poured out his love into our hearts by the Holy Spirit, whom he has given us.

God, I come before you today with a heart that's full of hope. You filled it to the brim today. There are days I feel so drained and disappointed. I care about people, so much so that sometimes I want to fix everything for them, Lord. I can't fix it, but thankfully *you* can. Help me to remember that I am a vessel. My heart is filled with love that you give me and show to me by the cross of your son, Jesus Christ. Help me today to give away the hope that you give me. My cup is never empty as long as your spirit renews my heart and your "hope supply" will never run dry.

Amen.

Psalm 51:10–12

Create in me a pure heart, O God, and renew a steadfast spirit within me. Do not cast me from your presence or take your Holy Spirit from me. Restore to me the joy of your salvation and grant me a willing spirit, to sustain me.

Oh God, this psalm stands alone as a prayer of renewal. It certainly doesn't need my words to make it more beautiful. My prayer today is for *my* heart, Lord. Create a pure attitude within its depths. As I am writing this prayer, it has just finished raining outside, the sun is shining, the air is fresh, and the earth is restored. May I remember this moment of restoration, even when the sun does not shine. May your Son shine in the dark days, oh God, so that your light enlightens my heart, my attitude, and my willingness to serve you. Thank you for the Son.

Amen.

Jeremiah 29:12–14

Then you will call upon me and come and pray to me, and I will listen to you. You will seek me and find me when you seek me with all your heart. I will be found by you, declares the Lord.

Lord, I'm so distracted today! From the things I should get done to the things I could get done—or would like to get done, if all the other people would do their jobs. Frankly, I'm paralyzed by the-should-a, could-a, would-a syndrome. Listen to me, Lord, I sound crazy. I desperately seek your guidance today. You promise to listen to me even when I rant and rave. I desperately need alone time with my heavenly Father, away from the hubbub, to gather my thoughts so that we can face and prioritize my responsibilities together. I can't handle this day alone, Lord. It's you and me, and I'm listening.

Amen.

Ephesians 3:14–19

For this reason I kneel before the Father, from whom his whole family in heaven and on earth derives its name. I pray that out of his glorious riches he may strengthen you with power through his Spirit in your inner being, so that Christ may dwell in your hearts through faith. And I pray that you, being rooted and established in love, may have power, together with all the saints, to grasp how wide and long and high and deep is the love of Christ, and to know this love that surpasses knowledge---that you may be filled to the measure of all the fullness of God.

Father, I cry out to you. I needed this passage so much today. I'm very down-in-the-dumps, but what this passage tells me is that the people on earth, along with the saints already in heaven with you, have all gone through the same stuff. The commonality we share is faith in you, Father. My little brain can't possibly grasp this geometry lesson you are trying to teach me. How wide, long, high, and deep *is* your love? It can't be measured, only felt in the depths of my heart.

I pray for strength from your Spirit, so that together we can make it through this situation. So here I am, Lord, on my knees. This is the best place I can be right now. I'm at my wits end, but your love knows no end. Where I end, you begin, rooted safely in my heart. I love you, Lord.

Amen.

Psalm 19:14

May the words of my mouth and the meditation of my heart be pleasing in your sight, O Lord, my Rock and my Redeemer.

Lord, my mouth, my words, my voice, my tone, or my language can make such a difference. Words of encouragement versus words of criticism, cheerful tone or an angry one, a language that's healing or cutting—the choice is mine. Yet once a word is uttered, it can't be taken back. This goes for making jokes, too. I like to smile and laugh, but please let it never ever be at the expense of someone's feelings. Help the words that I do verbalize to be heartfelt, positive, and pleasing to the people I encounter. Oh, and Lord, this language includes my self-talk as well. Cutting myself down is detrimental and unattractive.

May the words from my mouth be pleasing in your view,

Filtered through a heart that is honest, positive, and true.

Amen.

Psalm 28:7

The Lord is my strength and my shield; my heart trusts in him, and I am helped. My heart leaps for joy and I give thanks to him in song.

Lord God, you're my strength. Do I lean on you too much, Lord? I feel like all I ask for is help, and I forget to thank you. I am truly, truly grateful. You are always there, shielding me every day from the dangers along my way—those that I can see and those that are not so obvious. I thank you, Lord, for helping me through these pitfalls. Lord, you already know this, but I am not a singer. You have created me to be a writer. I offer this prayer-song to you.

Thank you for the sun today and a window to see it through.

Thank you for the friends I meet and for the work I do.

Thank you for the place I live and those who gather here.

Thank you, Lord, for health and home; so glad that you are near.

I am so grateful, Lord. My heart is joyful when I write down all the things with which you have blessed me. Thank you, Lord.

Amen.

P.S. What are you thankful for?

Psalm 33:11

But the plans of the Lord stand firm forever, the purposes of his heart through all generations.

Lord, what is your plan in all this? I am having troubles. Right now they seem so big and heavy, Lord, it takes my breath away. I feel squeezed between the needs of my children and parents. But this isn't a new problem. This has been going on since the beginning of time. The promise I hold onto is that *your* plans stand firm forever. It is the purposes of *your* heart that will prevail. Father, I come to you today praying for your wisdom. It has prevailed from the time we cry out our first breath, until we release our last sigh of life. You, oh God, have a mighty plan for each and every one of us. Help us never to forget this. Your purpose prevails through the good times and the bad, through the happy times and the sad. I stand firm in your promises because they last forever.

Amen.

Psalm 73:26

My flesh and my heart may fail, but God is the strength of my heart and my portion forever.

God, you are my portion. You give me the right amount at the right time, exactly when and where I need it. No matter what the situation, the forecast, my outlook—rain, shine, whatever—you know what's best. You know how strong my heart is, what it can take, and what it can't. I need nothing more, nothing less. I truly appreciate it all, Lord. I look around me right now. I have everything I need. I want to be satisfied with all you've graciously given me. In many countries I'd be considered wealthy. My home and land would be a mansion. That being said, help me, Lord, to be generous with what I *do* have. My heart is strong. I have my health. Sure, I have had my health challenges, but you, Lord, saw me through all of that. For this I also thank you, Lord. You were, are, and always will be in sole possession of my heart. Thank you, Lord!

Amen.

Psalm 90:12

Teach us to number our days aright, that we may gain a heart of wisdom.

Dearest God, number our days. I don't know how many I have, Lord, so I guess that means I need to make each day count, *every* one. Today, the leaves are bright yellow, fiery orange, and vibrant crimson—all set in the framework against a sky that is the bluest of blues. The green is fading away; slowly the earth is going to sleep, but only after a blaze of color. A warm, beautiful fall day was your gift today. It was spectacular. Help me to remember this beautiful autumn day in the heart of winter, so that I can appreciate its beauty. You are an amazing creator to have made all this with one brush stroke of your creative paint brush. I will carry the beauty of today in my heart so that tomorrow, when I remember it in my mind's eye I can count every day as a colorful blessing from you, Lord.

Amen (even if the days ahead aren't so colorful).

Psalm 109:22

For I am poor and needy, and my heart is wounded within me.

Why do certain people and situations hurt me so much, Lord? Why do I need to experience this? Why is my heart broken? I have nothing. No, wait. I only *feel* like I have nothing. What I need, Lord, is just to know you are near me. I have you. You never left. I have to pick myself up. Thanks for helping me up, Lord, and brush myself off. I'm picturing you wiping away my tears, Lord. You and I will face this together.

Amen.

Proverbs 2:1–6

My son, if you accept my words and store up my commands within you, turning your ear to wisdom and applying your heart to understanding, and if you call out for insight and cry aloud for understanding, and if you look for it as for silver and search for it as for hidden treasure, then you will understand the fear of the Lord and find knowledge of God. For the Lord gives wisdom, and from his mouth come knowledge and understanding.

God, I accept your Word in its entirety. I don't understand it all fully. It seems it has to do with the timing of when I read it. But sometimes you make the words jump off the holy pages (that's so cool!), and yet, there are other times when I need to quietly savor the words and meditate on them. Nonetheless, I treasure our prayer time together, Lord. My knowledge, understanding, and insight into you, oh Lord, is an investment. Unlike gold or silver that a thief can steal, I treasure you in my heart. No one can take that away from me, but I can choose to freely share my faith story with others and invest in them as well.

Amen.

Proverbs 3:5–6

Trust in the Lord with all you heart and lean not in your own understanding; in all your ways acknowledge him and he will make your paths straight.

Lord, this is one of my favorite passages. I trust in you, Father. No matter what lies ahead on this path of life, I know that you'll be there. Your presence is everywhere, all around me, in my work, home, car: you are everywhere. I can't run or hide from you. My understanding is limited; I just acknowledge your control and wisdom in every situation. I do not lean on worldly wisdom. No, I lean on you, Lord.

Amen.

Proverbs 7:1–3

My son, keep my words and store up my commandments within you. Keep my commandments and you will live; guard my teachings as the apple of your eye. Bind them on your fingers; write them on the tablet of your heart.

Holy one, I wish I could remember everything. I wish I didn't have to make so many lists, so many things to do, because there's only so much time in the day. Therefore, I will begin and end my day in prayer. Whatever happens in between, you, God, are in charge. I *will* remember that all day today.

Amen.

Ecclesiastes 3:11

He has made everything beautiful in its time. He has also set eternity in the hearts of men; yet they cannot fathom what God has done from beginning to end.

Lord, time means nothing to you. We measure it—you, Lord, do not. Young, old, or somewhere in between doesn't matter. As your children, we all have jobs to do, no matter what our age. You made us each uniquely beautiful from beginning to end. I can't understand it all, but I trust in you, oh God, with all my heart that the beginning and end, as well as everything in between, are all safely and gently held in your hands.

Amen.

Matthew 22:37

Jesus replied: "Love the Lord your God with all your heart, and with all your soul and with all your mind."

In my heart, that's where I start,

And in my soul, you're in control.

In my mind, that's where you'll find

The love of Jesus, my God.

Amen.

Luke 6:45a

The good man brings good things out of the good stored up in his heart.

Lord, this just *happened* to be my devotion this morning. I wrote this passage down and stuck it to my computer at work. The word 'good' is mentioned three times. How do I "store up" good things in my heart, Lord, so that I have good to give away? I feel so drained sometimes and I find achieving balance difficult because of so many demands from so many people and situations. Life isn't perfect or fair. Only you are, Father. I seek balance when I should just be seeking you. Lord, please be the fulcrum I balance on, the rock I cling to, and please be my center in this crazy, mixed-up world. Lord, everything about you is good. You are in my heart and mind. I carry your goodness with me everywhere, remembering your goodness of yesterday, embracing the goodness of today, and looking forward to a tomorrow filled with good things, too. Thank you, Lord.

Amen.

2 Corinthians 2:4

For I wrote you out of great distress and anguish of heart and with many tears, not to grieve you but to let you know the depth of my love for you.

Just when I think my tears are dried up, more come. But you, oh Lord, have provided me with one person who's with me through thick and thin, tears and laughter, for better or worse. You knew we'd be a perfect match, able to face this imperfect life together. He's my best friend, my sounding board, and confidant. We've been married twenty-five years (half our lives).I can't write the depth of my love for him on this page. Lord, I just want to thank you for this imperfect person who married imperfect me. But together—now, that's a perfect match!

Amen.

Hebrews 4:7

Therefore God again set a certain day, calling it Today, when a long time later he spoke through David, as it was said before: "Today, if you hear his voice, do not harden you hearts."

Psalm 95:7–8a

For he is our God and we are the people of his pasture, the flock under his care. Today, if you hear his voice, do not harden your hearts.

Today, Lord. David wrote the Psalms long, long ago, and then the writer of Hebrews quotes David hundreds of years later. Now I hear this Scripture ringing in my ears and heart today. Lord, all we've got is today. Let's make the most of it. May my heart be receptive and open to what you have to say to me.

Amen.

Hebrews 4: 12–13

For the word of God is living and active. Sharper that any double edged sword, it penetrates even to dividing soul and spirit, joints and marrow; it judges the thoughts and attitudes of the heart. Nothing in all creation is hidden from God's sight. Everything is uncovered and laid bare before the eyes of him to whom we must give account.

Lord, this passage at first seems brutal, yet I'm glad that nothing is hidden from you. No secrets. You see everything; it is all out in the open. When I come before you in heaven, I pray that I can be proud of how I've behaved, but Father, if there's something that isn't right between us, expose it, uncover my shortcomings, and shine the light of your salvation. For Jesus is the light of the world. He led a perfect life, and is theliving Word. Jesus is the active force. He knows the attitudes of my heart and the thoughts of my mind. If something needs to be eliminated, reveal it. If something needs to be added, then show me how, when, and where. You're the accountant of my very soul, Lord.

Amen.

Hebrews 10:22

Let us draw near to God with a sincere heart in full assurance of faith, having our hearts sprinkled to cleanse us from a guilty conscience and having our bodies washed with pure water.

God, please cleanse my heart; my conscience is bothering me, really bothering me. I have trouble accepting your forgiveness for my failure. I am picturing you sprinkling me with a shower of your forgiveness—pure, refreshing forgiveness. I don't deserve this, Father, but you tell me in this passage that I can be cleansed fully, completely, with no more guilt, no more beating myself up. I can forget, move on, and learn from it. I need to say, Amen! Knowing I am forgiven fully, completely.

Amen.

Genesis 6:5–8

The Lord saw how great man's wickedness on the earth had become, and that every inclination of the thoughts of his heart was only evil all the time. The Lord was grieved that he had made man on the earth, and his heart was filled with pain. So the Lord said, "I will wipe mankind, whom I have created, from the face of the earth---men and animals, and creatures that move along the ground, and birds of the air---for I am grieved that I have made them." But Noah found favor in the eyes of the Lord.

Lord, what's different today, compared to the time of Noah? The world seems a mess: finances, famine, family breakdown, fidelity in marriage, and foreclosures. Why don't you just send another flood? Because in Genesis 8:20–22 it says, "Then Noah built an altar to the Lord and, taking some of all the clean animals and clean birds, he sacrificed burnt offerings on it. The Lord smelled the pleasing aroma and said in his heart: 'Never again will I curse the ground because of man, even though every inclination of his heart is evil from childhood. And never again will I destroy all living creatures, as I have done. As long as the earth endures, seedtime and harvest, cold and heat, summer and winter, day and night will never cease.'" And you, oh Lord, keep your promises. Thank you.

Amen.

Deuteronomy 4:39

Acknowledge and take to heart this day that the Lord is God in heaven above and on the earth below. There is no other.

God, you are in control in heaven and on earth. I need to acknowledge this each and every day. Yes, I do have to be accountable for my responsibilities here on earth, but ultimately, I am responsible to you, my loving God and Lord. I will take this thought with me today on my journey and keep it safely in my heart.

Amen.

Deuteronomy 6:5

Love the Lord your God with all your heart and with all your soul and with all our strength.

Today was a tough day, Lord, and I have another tough day ahead of me tomorrow. I need strength, *your* strength to make it through. Sometimes my heart isn't in it, but I need to rest up, sleep well, and awaken to a new day and a new attitude. I love you, Lord. Help me to remember that you love me always. You don't give me what you and I can't handle together. It's you and I today, yesterday, tomorrow, and forever.

Amen.

Deuteronomy 8:2

Remember how the Lord your God led you all the way in the desert these forty years, to humble you and to test you in order to know what was in your heart, whether or not you would keep his commandments.

Forty years, Lord? A forty-year test? I think if I were alive back then, I'd complain to you about this. I'd get impatient, I'd mumble, complain, cry, and feel sorry for myself. Wait, that's exactly what I'm doing. Lord, I know what's in my heart: impatience! Your timing is perfect; you wear no watch on your wrist. Time, as I know it and how I measure it, means nothing to you. I empty my heart tonight to you, Lord. I'm spilling my guts. This is what is uppermost in my heart:

I identify it: worries, concerns, problems.

I acknowledge it; yes, life can be tough and unfair.

I get rid of it so that you, Lord, can fill my heart with joy once more.

Amen.

Deuteronomy 30:14

No, the word is very near you; it is in your mouth and in your heart so that you may obey it.

Some days as I read Scripture, certain words just jump off the page. (Okay, you noticed the heart theme.) The more I read, Lord, the more I get to know you better. Sometimes though, the passages go right over my head, and yet at other times, the message is simple and obvious. Does it have to do with *my* receptiveness and attention? Lord, help me to open the eyes and ears of my heart today so I can sense your nearness. In your name I pray.

Amen.

1 Peter 1:22b

Love one another deeply from the heart.

Lord, sometimes you give us situations that test us to trust you. The places we find ourselves in, especially the most difficult ones, we can only handle by relying on you. Life can give us some awful stuff that, in turn, can help us to truly understand others as they encounter similar situations. We are not in this life alone. We are meant to help one another. You put me in not one, but two situations today where I could offer assistance to folks who needed to hear how you, Abba, helped me. I've been through similar things in my life and I could bare my heart to them. Sometimes, when we laugh or cry together, I can try to show them how you, Father, helped me through difficulty. I feel honored to have opportunities in which I am used to help others in need. Thank you for the *chances* that I was involved in today. You are my rock, my steadiness, my comfort. If I am given the opportunity to bare my heart to others today, I pray that they see you there, and together we can endure whatever it is that comes our way. Thank you for today, but Lord, please be there in my tomorrow, too.

Amen.

John 14:1

Do not let your hearts be troubled. Trust in God. Trust also in me.

Father God, the word that jumps out to me from this passage is *let*. Do I let myself get worked up about things? Yes, Lord, I do. Do I not let go of issues that bother me? Yes, Lord, I do that as well. Do I need to let you handle my situation? Yes, Lord, I do. It's a trust issue, isn't it? I'm going to hand my troubled heart to you, Jesus. I'm not holding on to my troubles any longer. Yes, I'm handing them over to you, God. There—my troubles are safely in your hands. Now my hands and my heart are free. They are free to do what you, Lord, have planned for me today and always.

Amen.

Matthew 11: 28–30

Come to me, all you who are weary and burdened, and I will give you rest. Take my yoke upon you and learn from me, for I am gentle and humble in heart, and you will find rest for your souls. For my yoke is easy and my burden is light.

Jesus, help me to be gentle and humble like you. I am weary of carrying worry, and my knees are buckling under the weight of my burdens. I need to set this stuff down. There! My hands are empty. I'll fold them in prayer. My knees are wobbly. I'll kneel in prayer. My eyes are teary. I'll close them. You, Jesus, wipe my tears and calm my fearful heart. Can I just put my head on your shoulder and rest? Jesus, thank you. I feel refreshed after letting go of all that stuff I was carrying. I don't even know what all the fuss was about anyway. I'm so happy that I can come to you anytime, anywhere, with any concern I have, and you will listen to me.

Amen.

Colossians 3:15a

Let the peace of Christ rule in your hearts.

Mighty God, you rule. Let *your* peace flood my heart with peace. I've already had a flood of tears today, Lord. My heart was a cauldron of worry earlier, but now, Lord, you have calmed those turbulent seas into a peaceful river. My troubles haven't changed, Lord, but my attitude toward them has. Help me to keep this calmness. Lord, help me remember that you're in charge, you rule, you steer the ship. No matter what happens, no matter what the outcome, no matter how long this storm continues, I'm on your team, Captain. You lead; you rule my heart with peace.

Amen.

Romans 5:5

And hope does not disappoint us, because God has poured out his love into our hearts by the Holy Spirit, whom he has given us.

Spirit of God, you are like a surprise package that arrives in the mail. You are God's gift to us, and each of us has a gift given to us personally by the Spirit. It is to be used to bless the body of Christ, namely, the church here an earth. No disappointments. God gives everyone different gifts that are poured into us—right into our hearts by the Holy Spirit. It's the gift that keeps on giving. Thank you.

Amen.

Psalm 7:10

My shield is God Most High, who saves the upright in heart.

Yes, God, you alone are my shield, my defense, my ever-present helper at the ready whenever, wherever, and however I need you. Many days it takes all I can do to stay upright, but you shield me, Father. You are my defensive shield. You have also given me an offensive weapon: your Word. Lord, whenever I read my Bible, Satan flees because he knows your Word, your living Word, namely, your Son, Jesus, has totally and completely defeated the evil one. So, to whoever is reading these words, fling open the Bible. Study what our mighty God has done and is still in the process of completing. Stay upright, fight, and sleep tonight, knowing in your heart that you are saved.

Amen.

Psalm 116: 6–7

The Lord protects the simple hearted; when I was in great need, he saved me. Be at rest once more O my soul, for the Lord has been good to you.

Lord, when I look back, you've always been there. I look at the situation at hand. Is it troubling? Yes. Is this a new trouble? No. Is this something that has resurfaced? Yes. Will you help me now, Lord? Yes. "I will never leave you or forsake you." Never? My heart is confident of your goodness, Lord.

Amen.

Proverbs 16:9

In his heart a man plans his course, but the Lord determines his steps.

Lord,

I write.

I write lots of lists.

I accomplish what I can.

I cross things off my lists.

I throw away my lists.

I start another list.

On and on it goes.

Today, Lord, I give my list to you. May I accomplish only:

1. What you deem important.
2. What you plan for me.

May I step firmly into your plan, knowing that my feet are planted firmly on stepping stones and not stumbling blocks. You are the Rock, the Rock of my salvation. I trust every step to be taken today within your plan.

Amen.

Proverbs 14:10

Each heart knows its own bitterness, and no one else can share its joy.

Why are some people never happy, Lord? They are glum or mad or negative. I get weary of this attitude. I can't seem to be joyful around them. How do these folks get away with this bitterness? I don't want to catch this negativity bug. Lord, be my strength and shield. I must work side by side with these people. Lord, vaccinate me, as it were, with your immunity, your peace, your quietness. Help me remember that I am in the world, not of the world. I am only passing through on my way to your heaven. It will truly be wonderful. Until then, help me not to be bitter. I am better than that, because I have the joy of the Lord in my heart. Thank you.

Amen.

Hebrews 12:2–3

Let us fix our eyes on Jesus, the author and perfecter of our faith, who for the joy set before him endured the cross, scorning its shame, and sat down at the right hand of the throne of God. Consider him who endured such opposition from sinful men, so that you will not grow weary and lose heart.

Perfect
Perfected
Perfecting
Perfection
Perfects
Defects
Rejects
Regrets
Regroup
Regain
Gain
Gaining
Give
Giving
Forgiving
Living
Loving
Learning
Relearn
Return
Redo
Do over
Over
I'm over it.
How'd I do?
Perfect

Just playing with words here. I'm not perfect, but Jesus, you are. We work together to perfect my faith every day. I am a work in progress. Jesus is the only perfect one; enduring the cross was an impossible feat, but not for him. I will not lose heart because my heart belongs to Jesus.

Amen.

Jeremiah 5:23

But these people have stubborn and rebellious hearts; they have turned aside and gone away.

Lord, I'm sorry. I goofed up. I like to think that I am in control over something. That's where I'm wrong. You are in control, totally. Please, Abba, don't turn aside or go away. Soften my heart; break it, if need be. My heart and my will are yours.

Amen.

Proverbs 14:13

Even in laughter, the heart may ache, and joy may end in grief.

Lord, how can I be happy and sad at the same time? As my kids leave home, I'm happy for their independence, but sad for their absence. I'm happy for my clean house, but sad for my empty house. I'm happy in their adulthood with all the responsibilities that go along with it, but sad at the end of childhood that had few responsibilities. Well, Lord, we've set them on the right path. Tonight I pray for my husband and myself. We have done our best. You, Lord, have been there every step of the way, and you are not finished yet. Heavenly Father, watch over all your children and their parents, for you are directing their paths on the happy days and the sad ones, too. I know this in my heart because I am your child and you are my heavenly Father in whose holy name I pray.

Amen.

Psalm 16:9

Therefore my heart is glad and my tongue rejoices; my body also will rest secure.

Father, remind me again today how much security you provide. Finances, friendships, and health can all be in limbo sometimes, yet my heart is going to rest tonight in peaceful slumber, knowing full well that my security rests only in you. On my pillow I rest my head, knowing the worries of today are not welcomed here. Under my blanket, I am protected from whatever would cause me harm. I close my eyes, knowing that you, Father, listen to each and every prayer. Abba, tuck me in as I rest in you.

Amen.

Psalm 33:21

In him our hearts rejoice, for we trust in his holy name.

Holy God Almighty,
I do trust in you, through thick and through thin.
You always come through, whether I lose or win.
When life is a struggle and times are tough,
I don't want for anything; your love is enough.
My heart rejoices, no matter what's ahead.
No fear of failure, there's nothing to dread.
Be with me today as you've been in the past.
You're Alpha, Omega—the first and the last.
Rejoice in today; yes, that's what I'll do,
Because today's all we have, and I'll live it for you.

Amen.

Luke 12:29

And do not set your heart on what you will eat or drink; do not worry about it.

Worry, worry, worry. What does this accomplish? Absolutely nothing. Father God, worry is wrong. Help me not to wring my hands in worry, but instead, to fold them in prayer. Help me not to pace the floors, but to pace myself better. When I close my eyes to sleep, help me quiet allthe worrisome thoughts spinning around in this head of mine. I can do nothing right now to change anything. May I sleep tonight knowing that tomorrow is a new day, bringing me new challenges we can handle together.

Amen.

Luke 12:34

For where your treasure is, there will your heart be also.

Oh Lord, your love is without measure;
It's worth much more than any treasure.
This love cannot be bought or sold;
It is more precious than the finest gold.
It's not stored in banks
Where any thief can steal.
It's not by the luck of the draw
Or the spin of a wheel.
No, this treasure is free,
But it came at a price.
Jesus paid it in full because
He paid with his life.

Amen.

Psalm 49:3

My mouth will speak words of wisdom; the utterance from my heart will give understanding.

Father God, tonight my prayer is for clarity of thought so that the words I speak may be, well, truthful, insightful, spirit–filled, smart, witty, spontaneous, timely, and trustworthy. Okay, I am really getting carried away here, aren't I? I'd like to be wise, Lord. I yearn to learn more about your Word every day. May my heart be smart and my words be true, because all my wisdom comes from you.

Amen.

Psalm 139:23

Search me O God, and know my heart; test me and know my anxious thoughts.

Morning

Another test ahead today, Lord? Yikes, life is full of them lately. I'm slowly, ever so slowly learning that fear and anxious thoughts do not come from you. They come from the Enemy. I will not be held captive by this. The blood of Jesus Christ cleanses me totally. The chains are broken. Let's face today together.

Amen.

Evening

I really would like this test to be done within my life. You know what's in my heart. It seems to be racing along with my brain at one hundred miles per hour. Quiet my spirit; tomorrow, well, it's not here yet. My thoughts need to turn away from what ifs and toward what is. What I do know for sure, Lord, is that you have tomorrow firmly under control. What is my job? It is to rest tonight, knowing that your plan for my tomorrow is good.

Amen.

Psalm 27:8

My heart says of you, "Seek his face!" Your face, Lord, I will seek.

Lord, I saw your face today. I saw you in the frightened eyes of one of my patients. Help me to view everyone I encounter with the same gaze, as if you were looking at me through them, and vice versa. Someday, Lord, when it's my time to go to heaven, I will get to see your face and look into your eyes. Until then, Jesus, help me to look at people just like you see them: non-judgmentally and non-condemningly, for you look deeper. You look into their hearts.

Proverbs 12:25

An anxious heart weighs a man down, but a kind word cheers him up.

Lord, help me today to not carry around anxious stuff. When I'm anxious, my blood pressure goes up, my heart rate goes up, which in turn makes my heart have to work much harder at, well, life. So much energy wasted. Anxiety and fear do not come from you, Father. What does come from you is peace. Peace, yes, that's the word I'll keep in my heart today. As I go through my routine, help me share your peace with others by using kind words, not only to my family, friends, and coworkers, but to the person who cuts me off on the highway or sneaks ahead of me in line at the store. Peace be with me today, and peace be with whoever is reading these words. Peace.

Amen.

Matthew 18:35

This is how my heavenly Father will treat each of you unless you forgive your brother from your heart.

Heavenly Father, it's relatively easy to say you forgive someone, but not so easy to really forget the incident, whatever it may be. Today, Father, help me to remember how you forgive. You wash my sins away and separate them as far as the east is from the west. As I look at and listen to my fellow brothers and sisters at church, work, school, or at home, help me to see them all reflected in Jesus' eyes, as forgiven, not forsaken, accepted, not rejected, and saved, not scorned.

Amen.

Psalm 20:1–4

May the Lord answer you when you are in distress; may the name of the God of Jacob protect you. May he send you help from the sanctuary and grant you support from Zion. May he remember all your sacrifices and accept your brunt offerings. Selah. May he give you the desire of your heart and make your plans succeed.

God of Jacob, every day has troubles; this one was no different. Lord, you provided strength from people I did not expect it. Thank you. Today included things that ranged from the mundane to the seemingly insane. All these things seemed to align themselves into your purpose for my day. God, you are the same every day, be it crazy or boring. I can depend on your grace and patience to see me through. Your purpose is number one. May it always be my heart's number one desire to fulfill.

Amen.

Deuteronomy 11:18

Fix these words of mine in your hearts and minds; tie them as symbols on your hands and bind them on your foreheads.

Lord, I wish I had a brain that could memorize everything. I don't, however, and that's okay. The more time I spend in your Word, the more I get to know you. Certain passages seem to jump out at me at just the right time. In fact, Psalm 46:10, "Be still and know that I am God," has been in my devotions and quoted in a sermon four times in just the last week. This passage has been a favorite of mine for such a long time.Thank you, as this passage is one that is bound in my memory and its meaning is fixed in my mind.

Amen.

Jeremiah 15:16

When your words came, I ate them; they were my joy and my heart's delight, for I bear your name O Lord God Almighty.

Lord, eating is something we do every day and take it for granted. Food tastes better when you are hungry. And the feeling of being full after eating a great meal—there's nothing better. Today, Lord, I pray for those who do not experience fullness. There are many in this world that are homeless, poverty-stricken, or just down on their luck, who do not have enough to eat. These people can be found around the globe, in the United States, or just around the corner. Father, help me to be aware of hunger. I will not turn away; I will help. I won't ignore it; I will give. Lord God almighty, help me to be aware of any emptiness that I have the wherewithal to fill.

Amen.

Psalm 40:8

I desire to do your will, O my God; your law is within my heart.

Heavenly Father, what is it that you would have me do? Some days, I look around and the world seems to be falling apart. There is so much crime, catastrophes, violence, and corruption that it is hard to be a God–fearing person. So many in the world ignore, hate, or reject you. I don't, I won't, I can't ignore you. The rules I follow are in my heart. Not only are your commandments there, too, but the greatest one given by Jesus, "Love your neighbor as yourself," is also there. I need to remember this one each and every day, in every way.

Amen.

Proverbs 15:13

A happy heart makes the face cheerful, but heartache crushes the spirit.

Lord God, I do feel crushed in spirit tonight. Nothing terrible happened, no disaster, no loss. I'm just not in a happy spirit. I need to turn my frown upside down. I will sit here quietly in your presence for a couple of minutes. I will quiet my heart, regroup, refocus, refresh, and just give it a rest. Thus, I'll be refreshed by your spirit.

Amen.

Matthew 9:22

Jesus turned to her. "Take heart, daughter," he said, "your faith has healed you." And the woman was healed from that moment.

Jesus, it's like you are speaking right to me, aren't you? I wish I could have met you, seen you, witnessed your miracles here on earth, but I was born too late for that. I hope I have enough faith like the woman whom you healed. Lord, I need healing—spiritual healing. I am feeling very wounded in spirit at this writing, yet you tell me, Jesus, to "take heart and be healed." I will take heart, Lord. I will keep looking up, because as I look up into your face, I see my compassionate Savior who loves and heals me.

Amen.

Proverbs 4:23

Above all else, guard your heart, for it is the wellspring of life.

Lord, keep my heart beating in time with yours. May my will conform to your will as we travel together on the river of life. Sometimes the waters are rapid and turbulent, but sometimes it's smooth sailing. No matter where this river turns, you are with me. You never leave me nor forsake me; instead, you guard my heart. I will do my best to keep it healthy.

Amen.

Psalm 13:2, 5, 6

How long must I wrestle with my thoughts and every day have sorrow in my heart? How long will my enemy triumph over me?

Lord, why do I wrestle with my thoughts? I was thinking about things on the way to work this morning and wham! I started crying. What's up with that? I don't know where the tears came from, Lord. See what I mean? Wrestling. Why do all these thoughts swirl around in this head of mine? The Enemy—that's it. Sometimes the enemy is none other than me, myself, and I. verse 5 of this psalm contains the answer: "But I trust in your unfailing love, my heart rejoices in your salvation." And again in verse 6: "I will sing to the Lord, for he has been good to me." My heart will trust in you, Lord, and the goodness of your plan of salvation through your son, Jesus Christ. My heart rests in you, Lord. It seems that I'm crying and I'm rejoicing in the goodness you provide me every day. Thank you for clearing my thoughts, Lord, so I can see the Sonshine again.

Amen.

Philippians 1:7

It is right for me to feel this way about all of you, since I have you in my heart; for whether I am in chains or defending or confirming the gospel, all of you share in God's grace with me.

Lord, today I lift my friend, _____ to you. Bless his/her day, their work, their coming and going. This person is so near and dear to my heart. Lord, may my dear one be blessed today in spirit, deed, and body by your Holy Spirit, God. I pray this for my friend with all my heart.

Amen.

Ezekiel 33:31b

With their mouths they express devotion, but their hearts are greedy for unjust gain.

God above, look down on me today; hear me from heaven. May the words I utter please you, not just make me sound wise or look good. May my heart be open, not just to what this world has to offer, but to what I have to gain by knowing I am saved and heaven awaits.

Amen.

Psalm 57:7

My heart is steadfast, O God, my heart is steadfast; I will make music.

My God is steadfast. He is always there, just like my heart he created beating in my chest. He is constant and consistent like the beat of music, like the sound of a song, or like a beautiful voice singing and praising him. I have a song to sing in this very prayer that is from my heart.

Amen.

Psalm 125:4

Do good O Lord, to those who are good, to those who are upright in heart.

Sometimes I feel like my heart just plain falls down, sinks and hits the floor. Help me, Father, so I can walk upright again. I'm reaching out for you. Please grab my hand.

Please hold on tight.	"I won't let go, my child."
Lift me up.	"I'm holding on always."
Please, don't let go.	"Not on your life, never, ever."
Good?	"Good!"

I Love you.   "I love you, too."

Amen.

Psalm 27: 13–14

I am confident of this: I will see the goodness of the Lord in the land of the living. Wait for the Lord; be strong and take heart and wait for the Lord.

Lord, I am in need of confidence. I feel as if I'm getting criticism from every side and I take things far too personally. You tell me to wait, be strong, and then wait some more. Are you sure about this, Lord? Wait. Okay, wait. This is good; while I'm waiting, I'll pray. Calm my attitude. Calm my spirit with your Spirit. Let me know that your spirit of goodness surrounds me, no matter what. Help me to have faith in what I can't see right now. Oh Lord, guide me, so that I'm confident enough to take a step, even though I don't know what that next step is. Help me be your confident servant.

Amen.

Jeremiah 29:13

You will seek me and find me when you seek me with all your heart.

Father God, I sought you. I cried out to you quite literally, in fact. It's rather embarrassing how quickly my emotions took over my psyche, but you responded, oh Lord. You listened to me, and you heard me. You responded by providing me with wonderful friends. I received hugs, I heard expressions of "I love you," and they let me cry on their shoulders. I was looking for you, Lord, and I found you in the presence of friends who were present.

Amen.

Luke 8:15

But the seed on good soil stands for those with a noble and good heart, who hear the word, retain it, and by persevering produce a crop.

Father, still my heart today, so that it's resilient to the way

That life throws me curves, but I'll persevere,

Because through all the mayhem,

(You pick the line that best fits into you current situation:)

1. You are always near.
2. I have nothing to fear.
3. Your voice is all I hear.

Psalm 33:15

He who forms the hearts of all, who considers everything they do.

Holy God, I am created in your image. You knew me from the beginning of time. You knew what I would become and what I would do with my life. I am unique, but you create everyone to be unique. I may not be able to preach a sermon, lead a company, find a cure for a disease, or compose a symphony, yet I can write. Yes, Lord, I can write. And to you, whose eyes are reading this, you are gifted, too. He gave you a heart that is uniquely formed by his own hands. Use it to bless others, for in doing so, you will be a blessing in everything you do.

Amen.

Romans 10:9–10

That if you confess with your mouth, "Jesus is Lord," and believe in your heart that God raised him from the dead, you will be saved. For it is with your heart that you believe and are justified, and with your mouth that you confess and are saved.

Lord God, may the words that come out of my mouth today match what I believe in my heart of hearts: Jesus is Lord.

God raised him from the dead.

I proclaim this.

I believe this.

I am saved.

Amen.

Proverbs 12:25

An anxious heart weighs a man down, but a kind word cheers him up.

Father God, this Bible verse you pointed out to me is one I found in the newspaper today. It was in an article written by a financial planner about worry, of all things. I cannot believe how much I needed this today. I have many weighty concerns in my life. Actually, everybody does. I'm not unique, Lord. That being said, I need a kind word. What will be that word? How about *hope*?

I hope for a better tomorrow, Lord.

I hope to put a smile on someone's face.

I hope for a positive attitude.

I hope.

I am hopeful at the moment. The worry that was weighing me down doesn't feel so heavy now. I feel lighter in spirit. Thank you, Lord, for listening to me when I pray.

Amen.

Proverbs 24:17

Do not gloat when your enemy falls; when he stumbles, do not let your heart rejoice.

Father, I love to laugh. Let my jokes never be at someone else's expense—never. Let me laugh with people, not at them. Help me to laugh at myself sometimes as well.

Amen.

Song of Solomon 8:6a

Place me like a seal over your heart.

God, I wish I could seal out all the anxiety, frustration, tears, and worry that I have in my heart right now. Today I could not stop crying. I felt so embarrassed about this. Wait a minute. Place me (that's you, God) like a seal over my heart. Lord, I don't want to seal in the bad stuff. I need to give this worry to you, then, Lord, seal it. Place a stamp there. I'm yours, no one else's. My heart feels empty; I have cried all the tears I can. Lord, I ask you into my heart instead. Empty me of sadness and then fill me with gladness. Okay, that is kind of corny, but you know what? There is a smile on my face, the first one today. Thank you, Lord. You answered my prayer.

Amen.

Deuteronomy 6:4–9

Hear, O Israel: The Lord our God is one. Love the Lord your God with all your heart and with all your soul and with all your strength. These commands that I give you today are to be upon your hearts. Impress them on your children. Talk about them when you sit at home and when you walk along the road, when you lie down and when you get up. Tie them as a symbol on your hands and bind them on your foreheads. Write them on the doorframes of your houses and on your gates.

Lord, this was used as a text for a sermon I heard and it was very rich in meaning, powerful in motivation, and full of action. I see the word *command*. You, Lord, command me to not only keep these words in my heart, but they should energize me into action. Here are the verbs I hear: love, keep, recite, talk, bind, fix, and write. Being a writer, I especially like the last one. Thank you for your Word. Lord, I'll keep this in my heart today. May what's in my heart be visible to the outside, as evidenced by my actions.

Amen.

Deuteronomy 5:29

Oh, that their hearts would be inclines to fear me and keep all my commandments always, so that it might go well with them and their children forever!

God, I am your child, inclined not to listen. I have children who are inclined to not hear me. I am my parent's child, who was inclined to tune them out at my kids' ages, too. My heavenly Father, you always listen to me, not that you give me everything I want. No, you give me just what I need. To fear my heavenly Father means that I know he knows what's best for me. I trust that fact always, with my whole heart.

Amen.

Psalm 45:1

My heart is stirred by noble theme as I recite my verses for the king my tongue is the pen of a skillful writer.

Lord, you picked this passage just for me today, didn't you? Writing can be overwhelming, tearful, rewarding, honest, painful, brutal, precious, personal, and helpful. I know in my heart this is what I'm supposed to be doing. To whoever reads this, I have a question for you: "What is God telling you in your heart today? I'm praying from my heart for you all.

Amen.

Psalm 40:12

For troubles without number surround me; my sins have overtaken me, and I cannot see. They are more than the hairs on my head, and my heart fails within me.

Jesus, within me, my heart fails; beyond me are troubles too many to count. What would I do without you, Jesus? I'd be completely alone. I'm so glad you are within my heart, always taking care of me within your time frame, within your way, within your will. Thank you, Jesus.

Amen

Psalm 45:5

Let your sharp arrows pierce the hearts of the king's enemies; let the nations fall beneath your feet.

Jesus, you are my king. When you walked on earth, you had enemies. Judging by all the wars going on these days, Christians still have enemies. There are many religious conflicts currently raging in many parts of this world. Sometimes, Lord, the world just seems to be a mess. But you are my king. I pray today for all world leaders, especially in the United States. We have "In God We Trust" engraved on all our currency. I don't know, or even pretend to know about national issues, but you, Jesus, were a citizen on earth, just like I am. May I think about the ground beneath my feet today and appreciate freedom.

Amen.

Psalm 119:30

I have chosen the way of truth; I have set my heart on your laws.

Lord, there are the laws of nature, the laws of physics, and courts of law. There seem to be laws for everything. As a society, we would be in disarray and mayhem without the existence of laws. But Lord, your laws go beyond these earthly laws. Your creation follows your laws. We, the people you created, should follow the commandments, but we are human. We have faults and we fall short. Today, right now, I choose to follow *the* way—the way of truth. There is only the way, the truth, and the life. No one comes to the Father except by you, Jesus. (See John 14:6.) I choose you, Jesus.

Amen.

Romans 8:27

And he who searches our hearts, knows the mind of the Spirit, because the Spirit intercedes for the saints in accordance with God's will.

Holy Spirit,

Search my heart, for in there you'll find

A jumble of feelings plaguing my mind.

Quiet me, Spirit, and make me whole.

Fill me with hope that is the anchor to my soul.

Amen.

Psalm 37:4

Delight in the Lord and he will give you the desires of your heart.

Jesus, I am currently looking at my Christmas tree decorated with lights. I see through my window that neighbors' yards and houses are all decorated as well. But wait, it's December 21, the shortest day of the year. We seem to be in darkness, but the night you were born, Jesus, angels lit up the sky. Oh, how I wish I could have seen all that, including the tiny baby born in a humble manger. My heart delights in the Christmas story because you are the world's shining star giving light and hope to all. Praise your holy name, Jesus.

Amen.

Deuteronomy 6:5

Love the Lord your God with all your heart and with all your soul and with all your strength.

Oh God,

I don't feel very strong right now, but I love you anyway.

My soul is very sad, but I love you anyway.

I cried a lot today, but I love you anyway.

"I saved you my child, because I love you anyway.

I picked you up and held you close, because I love you anyway.

Even when you don't love yourself, I love you any way."— God

Amen.

1 John 3: 19–20

This then is how we know that we belong to the truth, and how we set our hearts at rest in his presence whenever our hearts condemn us. For God is greater than our hearts, and he knows everything.

God, my heart is open to you. You know everything. I can be totally honest with you. Honestly, Lord, I need rest. I feel like I have been going a billion miles an hour. I have to slow down. The truth is, I need help with this. I have been going so fast for so long, that I can't prioritize any more. Help me to get rid of the needless stuff, and only do what you, oh God, need me to do. Set my path, set my priorities, set my feet on the right way, and set my heart to know the truth. My heart belongs to you, oh God.

Amen.

2 Peter 1:19

And we have the word of the prophets made more certain, and you will do well to pay attention to it, as to a light shining in a dark place, until the day dawns and the morning star rises in your hearts.

Good morning to you, Lord. I love the morning, the hope of a new day. You, Jesus, are the star of Bethlehem. The wise men followed the star to you, a little baby who saved us all. Shine in my heart, Jesus; create light, and make the darkness flee from me. I will bask in the light of your salvation all day. May you, the morning star, fill my heart and attitude with light, because in your presence, there is no room for darkness.

Amen.

2 Corinthians 4:6

For God, who said, "Let light shine out of darkness," made his light shine in our hearts to give us the light of the knowledge of the glory of God in the face of Christ.

Blessed baby Jesus, how I wish I could sing *Happy Birthday* to you in a voice as lovely as the angels surely did so long ago. What I *can* do is use my gifts to praise you, so I'll continue to praise you with prayers, Jesus. Happy Birthday, my friend!

Amen.

Psalm 13:5

But I trust in your unfailing love, my heart rejoices in your salvation.

Dearest Savior,

I marvel at the manger, the star, and humble stable.

I will rejoice in my salvation, as long as I am able.

I wasn't personally there to see

Your lowly birth that night,

That's why I trust your love with all my heart

And live by faith, not sight.

Amen.

Psalm 46: 1–3

God is our refuge and strength, an ever present help in time of trouble. Therefore we will not fear, though the earth give way and the mountains fall into the heart of the sea, thought the waters roar and foam and the mountains quake with their surging.

God, sometimes it feels like this world is literally shaking and coming unglued. All one needs to do is read the headlines or watch the news and panic can overtake us. I know you are my refuge and strength. There are no other strongholds on earth. We must cast our eyes to heaven and take comfort in the fact that you, alone, are ever-present and everlasting. Nothing is outside your control. My heart rests in your refuge, my faith in your strength, and my help in you alone.

Amen.

Psalm 62:8

Trust in him at all times, O people; pour out your hearts to him, for God is our refuge.

Lord, sometimes I feel like I pour out my heart to you only during the bad times. I don't want to do that, because my heart is full and overflowing with good things. I want to tell you how thankful I am for dear friends and my family. I do love them so. I run to my friends and family for refuge. They listen. May I also listen attentively to them when they need me.

Amen.

Isaiah 26:8

Yes, Lord, walking in the way of your laws, we wait for you; your name and renown are the desire of our hearts.

Yes Lord, I want to be a "yes, Lord" person! That is what I desire. Your laws keep me walking straight. Your way is what I desire, and I will wait patiently for your plan to unfold.

Amen.

John 14:26–27

But the Counselor, the Holy Spirit, whom the Father will send in my name, will teach you all things and will remind you of everything I have said to you. Peace I leave with you; my peace I give you. I do not give to you as the world gives. Do not let your hearts be troubled and do not be afraid.

Holy Spirit, you have been given to us after Jesus ascended into heaven, and the gift you so freely give us is peace. It is here, it is real, and it is in our hearts. I need to be reminded of this every day. I wake up in the morning and I think about all the things I have to do. Why do I do that? Instead, I should get on my knees, fold my hands, and remember the gift that I already have: your peace. Nothing in this world provides us with the peace that surpasses all understanding.

I take a deep breath

And exhale slowly.

Today is new;

Yesterday is gone.

May I accomplish

What is on the Lord's to do list.

I let go of my troubles;

I let God do the trouble-shooting.

The Prince of Peace reigns in my heart

Today, tomorrow, and always.

Amen.

Isaiah 40:11

He tends his flock like a shepherd: He gathers the lamb in his arms and carries them close to his heart; he gently leads those who have young.

Gentle Shepherd, I love the thought of being gathered in your arms. As I have cradled my own children in my arms, so, Father, you hold me. A baby hears its mother's heartbeat before birth and afterward. When the mother rocks him to sleep, he rests against her chest and hears that soothing heartbeat again and again. Thank you, heavenly Father, for your gentle leading and guidance of my earthly family. Someday we will give each other a hug in heaven, but until then, I will give the people I love a lot of hugs today.

Amen.

Psalm 34:18

The Lord is close to the brokenhearted and saves those who are crushed in spirit.

Lord, there are days when I feel broken—not only brokenhearted, but just broken. As I get older, stuff that used to not hurt, hurts. I have aches and pains I never had when I was younger. I feel disappointed when things don't work the way they used to or the way I planned. The future looks dim. Okay, I've had my little feel sorry for myself, pity party. I'm done now. You, Lord, put a Band-Aid on my heart, even when I'm feeling sorry for myself. You love me when I'm un-lovable. Thank you for saving me in spite of myself.

Amen.

James 1:8

He is a double-minded man, unstable in all he does.

James 4:8

Come near to God and he will come near to you. Wash your hands, you sinners, and purify your hearts, you double-minded.

God, I don't want to be double-minded. Lately, it seems I can't make a decision. I want to stand firm one way, but I doubt. Yes, that's it, Lord, doubt. That's my trouble. Lord, wash my hands and heart of doubt. May I stand firm by coming near to you and your Word. You are my stability. The world may be crashing down all around me, but my heart and mind rest securely with you, Lord.

Amen.

Colossians 3:1

Since, then, you have been raised with Christ, set your hearts on things above, where Christ is seated at the right hand of God.

God up in heaven,

I raise my eyes up to look for you.

Where are you, Lord?

Above in heaven?

Jesus you have overcome death.

You were raised from the dead.

Where are you, Jesus?

"He is not here, he is risen," said the angels.

Jesus is seated at the right hand of God the Father in heaven.

I know in my heart this is true.

Amen.

Proverbs 15:14

The discerning heart seeks knowledge, but the mouth of a fool feeds on folly.

Father,

As I open my mouth today, be the gate-keeper of what I say.

Be beside me as I'm talking and on the path where I am walking.

May my words be fair and true, reflecting what I say and do.

Amen.

Proverbs 15:15

All the days of the oppressed are wretched, but the cheerful heart has a continual feast.

I am hungry. Not for food, but for a good attitude. Seems my good attitude has been stolen. I let people with negative attitudes, hungry for my good attitude, steal mine away from me. Lord, help me not to be a doormat. Feed my soul with goodness, Lord. Life does not always seem good, but the fact that I am living and breathing means I have a purpose. May I have a positive attitude today, no matter if the sun is shining or not. No matter what this day brings, I can control my attitude toward it. Help my heart to be truly cheerful.

Amen.

1 Samuel 16:7

But the Lord said to Samuel, "Do not consider his appearance or his height, for I have rejected him." The Lord does not look at the outward appearance, but the Lord looks at the heart.

Lord, you are my cardiologist of sorts. You don't need an EKG, blood work, or a stress test to know what's in my heart. You look with the eyes of my Lord, my friend. You examine me through loving eyes, not critical ones. It does not matter if I'm having a bad hair day or my clothes do not match. Those superficial things are not critical matters to you. Help me keep my heart healthy by knowing just how very much you love me.

Amen.

Philippians 4:7

And the peace of God, which transcends all understanding, will guard your hearts and your minds in Christ Jesus.

Jesus, I need your peace. We all need your peace! I do not understand why you love us so much, but you do. Your peace is a shield that stands guard around my heart and holds the thoughts in my mind captive, too. I love the fortress you've built around me. I feel safe and loved. You're the best, and I love you.

Amen.

Hebrews 12:2–3

Let us fix our eyes on Jesus, the author and perfecter of our faith, who for the joy set before him endured the cross, scorning its shame and sat down at the right hand of the throne of God. Consider him who endured such opposition from sinful men, so that you will not grow weary and lose heart.

Dearest Jesus, I won't lose heart because this passage is so incredible that I am writing prayers for it twice. You wrote this one just for me, didn't you? Well, no, then I wouldn't be sharing it again and again. Jesus, you are the author of our faith. You wrote the manual: it's the Bible and it's all about you. You endure at your Father's right hand in heaven. You endure the opposition from sinful mankind. You endure, even though we treated you horribly. You died for me on the cross. You are my Savior. I will never grow weary of saying this. I won't lose heart, Lord.

Amen.

Deuteronomy 4:29

But if from there you seek the Lord your God, you will find him if you look for him with all your heart.

What if I look and you're not there?

What if you're not listening to this heartfelt prayer?

What if I seek you and I do not find?

Is it all for naught? Am I out of my mind?

"No my child, you've got me all wrong.

I've been walking right beside you all along.

Calm yourself down, relax, and take my arm;

I'm keeping you safe from all kinds of harm.

I'm working in ways that you can't even see.

I don't wear a watch; time means nothing to me.

I know the number of hairs on your head.

If you seek my face first, you have nothing to dread.

So take a deep breath and continue this day,

Knowing I am with you every step of the way."

Psalm 27: 8

My heart says of you "Seek his face!" Your face Lord, I will seek.

Lord, I get so frustrated at times. I feel like I need to be told things over and over again like a little child. I'm stubborn. My heart is seeking your face, Lord, but how do I know what you're saying to me? Maybe I just need to sit here and listen.

Amen.

Philippians 4:7

And the peace of God which transcends all understanding will guard your hearts and your minds in Christ Jesus.

Jesus, the Christ,

Today I ask for you to guard my mind,

For I know that in the end, you I'll find.

You protected me from needless worry.

Thoughts flit through; I'm in too much of a hurry.

Help me to know in my heart what's best,

For its within your care that I'll find true rest.

Amen.

Jeremiah 29:13

You will seek me and find me when you seek me with your heart.

I look for you Lord, not with my eyes, but with my heart. Open the eyes of my heart, Lord, for I do want to see you, really see you today. Will it be in nature? Or in a kind gesture? Or in an encouraging word? I don't know, but I look forward to seeing you at work in my world today.

Amen.

Psalm 26:2–3

Test me, O Lord, and try me, examine my heart and my mind; for your love is ever before me, and I continually walk in your truth.

Oh Lord, here comes another test. Another trial, another challenge. I'm not afraid, though. I picture us walking arm-in-arm, side-by-side, step-by-step together through this. You know my heart and I know yours, for your love is ever before me. We'll pass this test with flying colors together.

Amen.

Proverbs 3:1

My son, do not forget my teaching, but keep my commandments in your heart …

(Here's how.)

Proverbs 3:3

Let love and faithfulness never leave you; bind them around your neck, write them on the tablet of your heart.

(Here's a passage to never forget.)

Proverbs 3:5–6

Trust in the Lord with all your heart and lean not on your own understanding; in all your ways acknowledge him, and he will make your paths straight.

(This needs no improvement from me.)

Amen.

2 Corinthians 4:6

For God, who said, "Let light shine out of darkness," made his light shine in our hearts to give us the light of the knowledge of the glory of God in the face of Christ.

Jesus, we will meet face-to-face in heaven someday. Then I'll look upon the face of God. I have no doubts that this day will come. In my heart I know heaven is my ultimate home. Earth is not. Until that day, may I walk in the light of the knowledge that I am a saved child of God, because Jesus died for me and for you, too.

Amen.

John 16:33

I have told you these things, so that in me you may have peace. In this world you will have trouble. But take heart! I have overcome the world.

Jesus,

You came to the world.

You overcame all fear.

You took over my heart.

You take away all fear.

What did you leave me with?

Peace.

Thank you.

Amen.

1 Timothy 1:5

The goal of this command is love, which comes from a pure heart and a good conscience and a sincere faith.

Lord God, I was lying here, ready to go to sleep, yet wanting a pure heart—one that has nothing to hide. You know my heart already. You know me well. I feel guilty a lot, probably more than I should, and I also worry about what people think of me. And as long as I'm getting this off my chest, I worry too much about what I should have done or could have done. It sounds kind of stupid now that I write this all down. Yet, I'm being sincere and I'm clearing the air, purifying my heart, as it were. I need to let this all go. I beat myself up enough, don't I Lord? I need to love myself because you love me. You created me to be who and what I am. Let's clear these worries out and start with a pure heart tomorrow.

Amen.

Psalm 112:4, 7

Even I darkness light dawns for the upright, for the gracious and compassionate man.

He will have no fear of bad news; his heart is steadfast, trusting in the Lord.

Lord, I'm really trying to have a steadfast heart right now. I feel like I'm hanging on by a little bitty thread. But I *am* hanging on. I'm stepping out. I don't know what's out there to hang on to. Here I go: a leap of faith.

You caught me. You never really let go of me, did you! That string I was holding on to? Well, you wove it into something good. I couldn't see that at the time; I was in the dark. Thank you for turning on the light of your love on this situation.

Amen.

Ephesians 5:19

Speak to one another with psalms, hymns and spiritual songs. Sing and make music in your heart to the Lord.

You don't have to be a musician to own a song in your heart.

You don't have to be a maestro; we all have a part.

Some sing up high and some sing down low;

Some have a fast tempo and others take it slow.

It makes no difference to God how we dance or sing.

Participation is the key; showing up is the important thing.

So come take your place, even if you can't sing two measures.

God sure loves your trying; it's your effort he treasures.

Ephesians 4:18

They are darkened in their understanding and separated from the life of God because of the ignorance that is due from the hardening of their hearts.

Father God, I never want to seem hard-hearted, never. Sometimes when situations are new to me, I become fearful. I am in the dark and separated from you. This is very uncomfortable for me. Shed the light of your grace on my situation, and then help me to move forward in grace, your grace. I want to live the life you have prepared for me. Be with me as I take the first step; my heart is yours—ready, open, and pliable.

Amen.

Psalm 112: 7–8

He will have no fear of bad news; his heart is steadfast, trusting in the Lord.

His heart is secure, he will have no fear; in the end he will look in triumph on his foes.

Hello Lord,

Is there something you need to tell me? Sometimes I feel I'm in the dark, yet I trust you completely in the situation. You know what you're doing. Your timing is perfect.

Amen.

Okay, it's just me again. I am so glad I have you to hold onto during troubled times. What do people do without you, Lord? My heart is truly secure in the fact that you have written the ending to my story.

Amen.

Psalm 28:7

The Lord is my strength and my shield; my heart trusts in him, and I am helped. My heart leaps for joy and I will give thanks to him in song.

Father, shield me today from what dangers come my way. Some I can see; others are invisible to me. No matter, because I am happy to be your child, protected in her Father's arms. I trust you absolutely, positively, completely, impeccably, unquestioningly, and forever.

Amen.

Matthew 6:19–21

Do not store up for yourselves treasures on earth, where moth and rust destroy, and where thieves do not break in and steal. For where your treasure is, there your heart will be also.

Here

Every

Allocated

In**V**estment

Ensures a

retur**N.**

True

Riches

Exist!

A

Secure

Val**U**e

Requires

Equity in heaven.

Proverbs 15:15

All the days of the oppressed are wretched, but the cheerful heart is a continual feast.

Lord, today I will smile at people and mean it! No frown will furrow my brow. Smiling is contagious. This is a good thing to pass on to others. Thank you for this reminder, Lord.

Amen.

John 16:33

I have told you these things, so that in me you may have peace. In this world you will have trouble. But take heart! I have overcome the world.

Jesus, I crave peace. Seems like many days are filled with running around, time schedules, routines, deadlines, rush, rush, rush! This is my world right now; I have a job to do. I will have troubles, I know that, but you, Jesus, have overcome the world. Take heart, you say? Okay, I will. I put my heart in your care.

Amen.

Psalm 4:4

In your anger do not sin; when you are on your beds, search your hearts and be silent.

God in heaven, I spent an hour lying in bed awake last night. I admit I was worrying about today. I was concerned about how it would turn out. Guess what? Today turned out fine. It was a full day, a busy day, but yes, all my worrying was for absolutely nothing. I am sorry; I know better, Father. You orchestrated my today perfectly. Yes, there were learning experiences along the way, but we searched for answers and we found them. You never leave us or forsake us. I will rest quietly tonight remembering this fact. Thank you, Lord.

Amen.

Psalm 77:6

I remembered my songs in the night. My heart mused and my spirit inquired.

Spending quiet time with you, Lord, is what I like to do,

Especially at night, for it's when my pen likes to write.

Sometimes I laugh out loud; at other times I weep.

No matter what is on my mind, I write it down before I sleep.

I don't always write in prose, but I like the way a rhyme

Sticks better in my memory; I like to keep in time.

In time with life and work and play,

I like to record how I see God in my day.

It might be in miracles, be they big or small,

But no matter what, God is there through it all.

Amen.

Matthew 9:22

Jesus turned and saw her. "Take heart daughter," he said, "your faith has healed you." And the woman was healed from that moment.

Jesus, you healed so many. All this woman in Scripture did was reach out, touch your robe, and she was healed. Jesus, I'm reaching out to you. I know I cannot touch your robe physically, but I can reach out in faith and pray, knowing in my heart that you will heal me. Thank you, Jesus.

Amen.

Philippians 4:7

And the peace of God, which transcends all understanding, will guard your hearts and your minds in Christ Jesus.

God, I don't get it. I mean that I don't understand it. I guess I'm not supposed to. But I want it, I crave it, and I pursue it: peace, your peace. It is a gift for all. I'm asking, Father, for your peace. How do I achieve this? I focus on the cross of Jesus the Christ, your Son, my Savior, my friend, my salvation. Your plan guards my heart and mind above and beyond anything I could imagine.

Amen.

Luke 8:11–12

This is the meaning of the parable: The seed is the word of God. Those along the path are the ones who hear, and then the devil comes and takes away the word from their hearts, so that they may not believe and be saved.

Jesus, I hear your Word. Please let it take root in my heart. May my heart be open and receptive; may it be fertile ground. Help me listen, Lord, truly listen to you. If only my heart had ears! Wait, if I sit here quietly, I hear my heart beating—a true miracle. I will be still, quiet, and listen.

Amen.

Luke 8:15

But the seed on good soil stands for those with a noble and good heart, who hear the word, retain it, and by persevering produce a good crop.

I love the smell of spring time, the blooming flowers, and the budding trees, all resulting from fertile soil that has maintained the roots during the winter. Lord, help the soil of my heart to be pliable, retaining your promise of spring and new life.

Amen.

1 Chronicles 28:9

And you my son Solomon, acknowledge the God of your father, and serve him with wholehearted devotion and with a willing mind, for the Lord searches every heart and understands every motive behind the thoughts. If you seek him, he will be found by you; but if you forsake him, he will reject you forever.

Lord, search my heart, examine my motives. It's like I'm asking you for an MRI or blood test or X-ray. I'm a results person; I like to know what's going on. You do know me. Lord, you know the number of hairs on my head. You know my thoughts. To get these tests I'm asking for done, I need insurance. Okay, here's my insurance card: my faith, my faith in a God who knows all and is in control of it all. My faith rests in my God, my Jesus, who is the Great Physician. You heal me.

Amen.

Ezra 1:1

In the first year of Cyrus king of Persia, in order to fulfill the word of the Lord spoken by Jeremiah, the Lord moved the heart of Cyrus king of Persia to make a proclamation throughout his realm and put it in writing ...

Praise you, God! I am no king, queen, or anybody out of the ordinary. If you, Lord God, can move the hearts of kings, then you can move mine, too. I love to write. Maybe you, the reader, love to sing, dance, paint, build, sew, cook, clean, fix, or teach. Whatever you do let the Lord move into your heart today. Then watch what you both can accomplish.

Amen.

Psalm 73:1

Surely God is good to Israel, to those who are pure in heart.

Lord, a friend of mine's mother who was entering the final days of her journey here in earth, always signed off on her Caring Bridge entries with the phrase, *God is Good.* She is with you in heaven now. She knew your true character. She had a pure heart. God, you are so good. This may sound silly, but as I reflect on my loved ones who are with you, until I get there, Lord, give them a hug for me, will you? You are so good.

Amen.

Psalm 73:13

Surely in vain have I kept my heart pure; in vain have I washed my hands in innocence.

Jesus, Pilate washed his hands, as if to say, "I claim no responsibility for putting this innocent man, Jesus, to death." And you, Jesus, spoke the words while on the cross, "Forgive them Father, for they know not what they do." I'm praying to you right now to ask, "Forgive me, Lord." Your suffering and death happened over two thousand years ago, yet your death and resurrection have made it possible for me to receive true forgiveness. I cannot ever repay this debt. I come to you empty, asking for forgiveness: Purify my heart, Jesus.

Amen.

Psalm 73: 21–26

When my heart was grieved and my spirit embittered, I was senseless and ignorant; I was a brute beast before you. Yet I am always with you; you hold me by my right hand. You guide me with your counsel, and afterward you will take me into glory. Whom have I in heaven but you? And earth has nothing I desire besides you. My flesh and my heart may fail, but God is the strength of my heart and my portion forever.

Almighty One,

As I fumble around in this life,

You hold me by the hand.

As I look for answers,

You hold me by the hand.

As I fail or succeed,

You hold me by the hand.

As I learn something new,

You hold me by the hand.

As I face each challenge in faith,

You hold me by the hand.

When I don't know what's next,

You hold me by the hand.

When I lose the strength to move on,

I'll hold you by the hand.

When the day comes when heaven draws near,

I'll hold you by the hand.

Help me have the strength in my heart.

I'm holding you now and forever, my child.

2 Corinthians 4:16

Therefore we do not lose heart. Though outwardly we are wasting away, yet inwardly we are being renewed day by day.

Some days it's tough to even get out of bed,

To face the day, not knowing what's ahead.

One step at a time, not two or four,

Just one, that's all; we shouldn't take more.

We get ahead of ourselves and forget to renew.

A prayer's what's required; it's all we need do.

Will you join me today and take a new point of view?

You pray for me and I'll pray for you.

Our God's always listening; our prayers never bother.

In fact, he loves it when we pray for each other.

So take heart, my friend, because today's the day.

Let's forget our troubles, but remember to pray.

Amen.

Habakkuk 3:16

I heard and my heart pounded, my lips quivered at the sound; decay crept into my bones, and my legs trembled. Yet wait patiently for the day of calamity to come on the nation invading us.

Savior, when I look at the news headlines, this Old Testament prophet could have lived today. You, sovereign Lord, are my strength when I am weak. I am filled with joy when the earth seems to be crumbling, because my strength comes from my sovereign Lord. I will wait patiently while my heart beat slows, and no more pounding beats in my ears. I only am tuned into my Lord's voice. Be near to me. I am listening with a quiet, open heart.

Amen.

Colossians 3:15

Let the peace of Christ rule in your hearts, since as members of one body you were called to peace. And be thankful.

Jesus the Christ, you reign as king. You rule in peace. Worries have no place in my heart. Help me to build up others in my church community as we go about our lives. You call me to be a peaceful citizen while I'm here on earth. Even though this is only my temporary home, help me make the most of it. Make me a fellow peacemaker while working together in, with, and through the body of Christ—my church.

Amen.

Psalm 44:21

Would not God have discovered it, since he knows the secrets of the heart?

God, you knew the secret I had, though it was well hidden in my heart. I was concerned about some test results. I knew this situation was already in your hands, but I chose to waste energy and be worried about something I couldn't change. This was silly. Yet in it all and through it all, the result was positive, so much so that my heart was bubbling over with thanks to you, my Lord.

I praise you.

I thank you.

I love you.

Amen.

Job 15: 12–13

Why has your heart carried you away, and why do your eyes flash, so that you vent your rage against God and pour out such words from your mouth?

Father God, tonight I do have rage in my heart. I'm angry and disappointed about what happened today. Am I supposed to stuff this all inside and turn the other cheek so that someone can hit me there, too? How much am I supposed to put up with? Well, today is over, finished, done; I can do nothing to change it. What I do have control over is my attitude toward tomorrow. It will be a new day, a blank piece of paper, with no writing on it—a clean slate. I will make tomorrow better. Can you help me with my outlook, Lord? Because I know you are looking out for me.

Amen.

Ephesians 3: 16–18

I pray that out of his glorious riches he may strengthen you with power through his power through his spirit in your inner being, so that Christ may dwell in your hearts through faith. And I pray that you, being rooted and established on love, may have power, together with all the saints, to grasp how wide and long and deep is the love of Christ.

Dear Jesus, you do answer prayer. I heard from a friend today how you answered our prayer. There is power in spending time with you in quiet meditation, yet sometimes, this can turn into a tearful event. That does not matter; my heart is full of gratitude for your working in this situation, Lord Jesus. We can only imagine how wide, deep, long, and high your great love for us is. I want to throw open my arms and give you a hug. Oh yes, you worked with and in this situation and made it turn out wonderfully. Thank you, Jesus.

Amen.

Acts 16:14–15

One of those listening was a woman named Lydia, a dealer in purple cloth from the city of Thyatira, who was a worshiper of God. The Lord opened her heart to respond to Paul's message. When she and the members of her household were baptized, she invited us to her home.

God, I'm so glad I'm free to worship you openly in my home and community, unlike the early Christians when Paul was evangelizing. Keep my heart open, Lord. There is still much work to be done, at this time. Help me to be a living witness through the way I live and the words I speak, because I may run into somebody who needs me to respond and who needs to hear you, Lord.

Amen.

Deuteronomy 4:9

Only be careful, and watch yourselves closely so that you do not forget the things your eyes have seen or let them slip from your heart as long as your life. Teach them to your children and to their children after them.

Memory

I have trouble remembering many things, it seems, be they passwords or birthdays. As I am getting older, it takes a wee bit more time to recall things. Maybe it's because my time is so full of distractions. Help me to keep my quiet time with you as a precious priority each and every day. I do so enjoy our quiet time talking to each other, Lord. I will not let these moments slip away. I hope my kids remember me praying with them, and I hope I can start this tradition with my future grandchildren as well.

Amen.

1 Samuel 1:13

Hannah was praying in her heart, and her lips were moving but her voice was not heard. Eli thought she was drunk

Heavenly Father, sometimes I pray out loud to you on my way to work. I'm sure people think I'm singing to the radio or talking on the phone, but I find this to be a great time to talk to you. We had a snow storm overnight and it was still snowing this morning on the way to work. I thank you for your protection, Lord. I made it to and from work safely. Nothing will stop me from praying to you, Lord. I will continue praying in my heart every day.

Amen.

Exodus 35:21

And everyone who was willing and whose heart moved him came and brought an offering to the Lord for the work on the Tent of meeting, for all its service, and for the sacred garments.

Lord, sometimes I look around me and see so much need. There are charities for every disease, foundations established for need, and organizations for disasters. How do I apportion my resources? It feels good to give, but I can't give to everyone. Lord, motivate my heart to give, not only my resources, but my time, too. Prioritize my work for church and community.

Amen.

Isaiah 26:8

Yes, Lord, walking in the way of your laws, we wait for you; your name and renown are the desire of our hearts.

Lord,

You call me by name—

A personal invitation.

I treasure our friendship—

A personal relationship.

Be the curb to my life's path—

A personal trainer.

Amen.

Ezekiel 36:26

I will give you a new heart and put a new spirit in you; I will remove from you your heart of stone and give you a heart of flesh.

Getting a heart transplant is a radical thought to me. But I need it, don't I, Lord? Our hearts get broken through relationships, loss, and disease. You created us and molded our being. Keep our hearts in shape and flexible, so we can handle this life together.

Amen.

Exodus 4:21

The Lord said to Moses, "When you return to Egypt, see that you perform before Pharaoh all the wonders I have given you the power to do. But I will harden his heart so that he will not let the people go.

Lord, would I have been as courageous as Moses? You asked him to do something that he knew that the answer was going to be no.

So why did he even ask? Simply, because you, oh Lord, told him to. Moses just didn't ask questions; he just did it anyway. Obedience was the answer—not yes or no. Yours is the power, Lord, and to you be the glory. Everything in this situation is under your holy control. May my heart be this obedient.

Amen.

Psalm 119:2

Blessed are they who keep his statutes and seek him with all their heart.

Lord, today I looked for you; I looked high and low and all around. I didn't see you, but I heard you instead. Yes, I heard you, Lord. Someone asked me for a little help, a simple request really. Nothing big, yet I could fulfill that request. I felt needed. I thank you, Lord. I listened and I followed through. I heard you in my heart. I'm so glad you are always there with every heartbeat.

Amen.

Psalm 119:7

I will praise you with an upright heart as I learn your righteous laws.

Dear Lord, today I stand with an upright heart. I pray for attentiveness and receptiveness to all that you have to teach me. Put me in places where I can be a mirror and reflect your love. May I pay attention to the little things so that my actions and words are a source of praise to you, whenever, wherever, and however I am able. I praise you, Lord.

Amen.

Psalm 119:10

I seek you with all my heart; do not let me stray from your commands.

God in heaven, I felt pulled in many directions today. How do I not stray from the path you intended me to be on? I seek your face, I face the facts, I face reality, and I face what I have coming in the future. I seek your face. You, Lord, smile at me and hold out your hand. I look at your countenance; it shines. Psalm 27: 8 says, "My heart says of you, 'seek his face.' Your face Lord I will seek." I will not stray when you, Lord, show me the way.

Amen.

Psalm 119:11

I have hidden your word in my heart that I might not sin against you.

Dearest God, your Word is flawless. (Psalm 18:30:"As for God, his way is perfect; the word of the Lord is flawless.") I'd hope that I am flawless, too, yet I am a work in progress, aren't I? Life is, well, complicated. Yet your promises are written in Scripture, for me to read, heed, and succeed.

Amen.

Psalm 119:34

Give me understanding, and I will keep your law and obey it with all my heart.

Father God, I know I can ask you for wisdom and you answer. You give me friends and situations that challenge me, Lord. They make me think. They make me pray; now I'm on my knees asking for understanding. I get it, Lord: true wisdom is seeing you work through others, not to toot my own horn, but to play along in the orchestra of life. Sometimes I need to be in the harmonies in the background supporting the soloist. I am not the soloist today, Lord. Help me to play my part that you have assigned me with all my heart and to the best of my ability.

Amen.

Psalm 119:36

Turn my heart toward your statutes and not toward selfish gain.

Lord, when I die and go to heaven, I'd like to be remembered on earth for doing good things; I do not want to be remembered as being selfish. Oh, that thought pains me I do so want to be a giver and not a receiver. You, oh God, have blessed me with so much. Help me to share what you have given me, to be aware of the needs of others, and to care deeply with my heart. I can't fix it all, but I can fix my attitude to be in alignment with your statutes. Help me, Lord, to never turn my face away, but to face issues of need head on.

Amen.

Psalm 119:58

I have sought your face with all my heart; be gracious to me according to your promise.

Dear Jesus, I really wish I could see your face, yet I will see it when I go to heaven. Until then, I just wanted to let you know that I saw your face three times today. I saw you in the face of a homeless man I gave some change to, in the eyes of a nervous patient I took care of, and lastly, I heard you, Lord, in the encouraging words of a friend. Yes, Jesus, you promised me that I will see you in heaven, but until then, I promise to do the work you have set before me today.

Amen.

Psalm 119:69

Though the arrogant have smeared me with lies, I keep your precepts with all my heart.

God, sometimes I try to care. For eight hours a day, my place of employment pays me to care. I do my best at my job, I really do, but what do you do when somebody—a total stranger—treats you poorly? That person used words that I can't even write down here, yelling at me for something I was not responsible. I feel horrible, Lord. I'm crushed and tearful. I'm laying my hurts before you, oh God. Hold me; hold my broken heart and make it whole again.

Amen.

Psalm 119:111

Your statutes are my heritage forever; they are the joy of my heart.

Lord, I am going to have a lot of questions when I get to heaven. I do not question my faith. No, not that. My question has to do with heritage—my family, parents, grandparents, great-grandparents, and great-great grandparents who brought me up in the Christian church. Thank you, ancestors. There are many churches that go back generations like mine. Which one's right? Are we all right? All wrong? I don't know. What I do know is this: Jesus Christ died on the cross for me (and for everyone). That fact forever gives me joy in my heart, and I never question it.

Amen.

Psalm 119:112

My heart is set on keeping your decrees to the very end.

Yahweh, you know my (our) days are numbered. You know the exact number of days I have left. Let's make every one of them count. I don't know when I'll be called to heaven, but I do know that it will be like a reunion of all the saints who went before me. I look forward to that day, but until then, I will keep my heart set on doing my best with your help.

Amen.

Psalm 119:145

I will call with all my heart; answer me, O Lord, and I will obey your decrees.

Lord,

I do not need the internet or a phone to reach you.

I call out in prayer.

I never get disconnected, hear a busy signal, or pay roaming fees.

Thank you, Father, for just being a prayer away every day.

Amen.

Psalm 119: 161

Rulers persecute me without cause, but my heart trembles at you word.

I feel persecuted today, Lord. I had a particularly bad time of it. I was betrayed and yelled at for something that was not in my control. For once, could I be a hero instead of a zero? Okay, the pity-party is over; shake it off. Tomorrow is another day. Thank you for listening to my ranting and raving, Lord.

Amen.

Luke 16:15

He said to them, "You are the ones who justify yourselves in the eyes of men, but God knows your hearts. What is highly valued among men is detestable in God's sight.

God, help me not to care about how the world sees me, but to know that what is truly important is how you view me. You see my heart, Lord. What others see and the way I compare to them makes no difference to you. You see what is right. People see what is wrong. God values all people. We, in turn, should value each other.

Amen.

Isaiah 57:15

For this is what the high and lofty One says---he who lives forever, whose name is holy: "I live in a high and holy place, but also with him who is contrite and lowly in spirit, to revive the spirit of the lowly and to revive the heart of the contrite."

Oh Lord, I need a bit of revival right now. I've been beaten down and it's time to let go of what's dragging me down. Instead, I will hold on to your promise of revival and renewal. It's a new day.

Amen.

Mark 8:17–19

Aware of their discussion, Jesus asked them, "Why are you talking about having no bread? Do you still not see or understand? Are your hearts hardened? Do you have eyes but fail to see, and ears but fail to hear? And don't you remember? When I broke the five loaves for the five thousand, how many basketfuls of pieces did you pick up?

Jesus, the disciples had you personally to teach them. They heard your words, saw your miracles, and felt you calm the seas. I'm jealous in a way. Yet as I read this passage, I get the feeling you were a bit frustrated with the lot of them. Frankly, Jesus, I am glad I have perspective; I can look at the four gospels, read the stories, and imagine a picture of you in my mind. I understand the disciples. I probably would have had the same feelings they did. But Jesus, I can speak with you in prayer. Please, Jesus, don't let my heart be difficult and hardened. Help my eyes see where I can be of assistance, my ears be hear your suggestions, and my heart be understanding and responsive. I will remember this today, Jesus.

Amen.

Psalm 62:8

Trust in him at all times, O people, pour out your hearts to him, for God is our refuge.

God,

I take refuge in your loving arms, Father.

You provide protection like no other.

I felt unjustly treated today.

I think I'm supposed to turn the other cheek—really?

This is far easier said than done.

I need to forgive and forget.

Give me a minute;

This is difficult.

I pray for those who offended me,

I really do.

I'm unburdening my heart by pouring out my situation to you.

You listen.

You lift my burdens, wrap them in your grace, and take them away.

I'm picturing this all.

My heart feels lighter, freer, unburdened.

Thank you for your never-ending grace.

Amen.

Philemon 1:20

I do wish, brother, that I may have some benefit from you in the Lord; refresh my heart in Christ.

Just as I use the refresh button on my keyboard, I wish I had one I could use on my attitude, Lord. It would be a magic button I could press that would make my attitude new, my head bright with clarity, and my eyes open only to the good in people. Today, Lord, make it a refreshing day.

Amen.

Colossians 2:2

My purpose is that they may be encouraged in heart and united in love, so that they may have the full riches of complete understanding, in order that they may know the mystery of God, namely Christ.

Dear Jesus,

Thank you for today.

Thank you for whatever comes my way,

Because I do know that you are with me, no matter what.

It may be a bad day.

That's okay; it will make me stronger.

It may be a ho-hum day.

That's okay; I know you are still at work, cheering me on from the sidelines.

Or perhaps it will be a stellar day, off the charts—

The kind of day where I can say, "Amen, sista (or brotha)."

No matter what, Lord, I am encouraged to see what's ahead.

Amen.

Ephesians 6:6–7

Obey them not only to win their favor when their eye is on you, but like slaves of Christ, doing the will of God from your heart. Serve wholeheartedly, as if you were serving the Lord, not men.

What if I lived today as if you were my boss, my coworker, or someone I supervise?

Would my attitudes or actions change?

What if I lived today as if you were driving the car next to me, or standing in the checkout line at the grocery store?

Would I be as impatient as I usually am?

What if today was my last day on earth?

I'd better stop asking all these questions, Lord, and focus on living wholeheartedly today.

Amen.

Ephesians 5:19

Speak to one another with psalms, hymns and spiritual songs. Sing and make music in your heart to the Lord.

Lord, I am no musician, but I do love music. From the old hymns to gospel choirs, from Bach to the Beatles to Brubeck—I love it all. From revival tents to cathedrals to campfires in the woods, wherever there are hands to be raised, there are voices to sing your praise. You don't even care if all the notes are in perfect tune, do you, Lord? Music flows through the Spirit and into our hearts. May I keep this prayer-song in my heart all daylong.

Amen.

2 Corinthians 9:7

Each man should give, what he has decided in his heart to give, not reluctantly or under compulsion, for God loves a cheerful giver.

As the offering plate goes by, Lord, help me to remember that you gave me everything in the first place. Giving freely of my time and talent, as well as my riches, is a goal I've set for myself. On every penny, nickel, dime, quarter, and bill, the words *In God We Trust* are printed. As I trust you with my finances, I feel a secure freedom wash over me. The world can't give me this peace. It only comes from trusting in you, Lord.

Amen.

John 12:39–40

For this reason they could not believe, because, as Isaiah says elsewhere: "He has blinded their eyes and deadened their hearts, so they can neither see with their hearts, nor turn---and I would heal them." (See Isaiah 6:10.)

God, I do not fully understand the passages you put before me. So you explained it twice in the gospel of John, who quotes from the book of Isaiah written 680 years earlier. I know my eyes don't see like they used to. My heart has a few miles on it. My ears, well, they hear just fine, but they don't always listen. I guess I needed to read your Word twice to pray for healing. Heal me, Lord. I wrap my entire imperfect, aging (but still useful) self in your grace, because my faith rests securely in an ageless, timeless, healing God.

Amen.

Proverbs 17:22

A cheerful heart is good medicine, but a crushed spirit dries up the bones.

Creator God, you made us 60 percent water. The earth is covered by 70 percent water, and a human can only live three to five days without water. I have felt crushed lately—crushed in spirit, that is. You, Jesus, provide me with living water. Refresh and rejuvenate me in body, mind, and spirit. I long for a cheerful attitude, but negativity squelches it. Keep me hydrated and healthy in the living water of your Word.

Amen.

1 Kings 8: 23–24

O Lord, God of Israel, there is no God like you in heaven above or on earth below—you who keep your covenant of love with your servants who continue wholeheartedly in your way. You have kept your promise to your servant David my father; with your mouth you have promised and your hand you have fulfilled it—as it is today.

Lord God, there is certainly no God like you. You keep your covenant of love with us. You keep your promises. What you say is put into action—no hesitation, wavering, or variance. You have always been and always will be. You have kept your word in the past. You know what the future holds. Your promises are fulfilled.

Amen.

2 Corinthians 1: 21–22

Now it is God who makes both us and you stand firm in Christ. He anointed us, set his seal of ownership on us, and put his Spirit in our hearts as a deposit, guaranteeing what is to come.

Oh God, my money on earth means nothing really, because you, Lord, have made a guaranteed deposit of your spirit in the bank of my heart. No matter what happens, I stand firm in my faith, knowing that my fate is guaranteed forever.

Signed

In the manger in Bethlehem.

Sealed

On the cross at Calvary.

Delivered

At the empty tomb on the third day.

Amen.

Ecclesiastes 6:2

God gives a man wealth, possessions and honor, so that he lacks nothing his heart desired, but God does not enable him to enjoy them, and a stranger enjoys them instead. This is meaningless, a grievous evil.

God, you give us what we need. We lack for nothing. It sounds like this man in Ecclesiastes had everything he wanted. He had more than what he needed. Maybe he wasn't thankful; maybe he wasn't grateful. Scripture does not say. Heavenly Father, today and every day, I thank you for realizing the need to possess an attitude of gratitude toward possessions, people, and priorities.

Amen.

Psalm 140:1–2

Rescue me, o Lord, from evil men; protect me from men of violence, who devise evil plans in their hearts and stir up war every day.

Lord, there are people who stir up war around me every day. There are people who seem to love conflict. I'm not one of them. Help me today to have a peaceful heart, one that looks for good in others, not evil. All you have to do is look at the headlines and realize what an evil place this world is. But earth is now my home. Father God, protect my family and me from the violent world that surrounds us. I peacefully pray in your name.

Amen.

Zechariah 12:5

Then the leaders of Judah will say in their hearts, "The people of Jerusalem are strong, because the Lord Almighty is their God."

God, today I pray for leaders—leaders of countries, churches, businesses, and households. They have a very important role. With a strong heart and with you as their leader, they can accomplish much. If there is dissension in the ranks or doubt in their plans, life can surely crumble into chaos, but we, the people of God, are strong. Lead us, Father; be the strength of leadership's faith. May their bodies, minds, and spirits work together to accomplish much for the kingdom of the Lord.

Amen.

Matthew 9:1–3

Jesus stepped into a boat, crossed over and came to his own town. Some men brought him a paralytic, lying on a mat. When Jesus saw their faith, he said to the paralytic, "Take heart, son; your sins are forgiven."

Prayer for the beginning of your day:

Jesus, your ministry days on earth were very busy. You healed people, performed miracles, taught, and fed the crowds who followed you. But most importantly, you forgave people—something that no one else but you could offer. Jesus, as I navigate through my busy day, help me to keep forgiveness in my heart. From my commute on the highways to my interaction with coworkers, let my heart be forgiving.

Amen.

Matthew 9:4–7

Knowing their thoughts, Jesus said, "Why do you entertain evil thoughts in your hearts? Which is easier: to say, your sins are forgiven, or to say, "Get up and walk? But so that you may know that the Son of Man has the authority on earth to forgive sins ...." Then he said to the paralytic, "Get up, take your mat and go home." And the man got up and went home. When the crowd saw this, they were filled with awe; and they praised God, who had given such authority to men.

Prayer for the end of your day:

Jesus, today was a tough one, but we made it, didn't we? We faced a lot of frustrations, yet there are many good people out there who are striving right along with us on this path of life. Tonight, as my head hits the pillow, I know in my heart that I am a forgiven child of God, healed inwardly and outwardly by my Savior and friend, Jesus.

Amen.

Galatians 4:6

Because you are sons, God sent the Spirit of his Son into our hearts, the Spirit who calls out, "Abba, and Father."

Abba, Daddy, Abba!

I call out to you as a child needs her parent.

When I am scared,

You are there, Abba.

When I am unsure of what to do next,

You are there, Abba.

When I want to scream,

You are there, Abba.

When my heart overflows,

You are there, Abba.

Is there any place you are not, Abba?

No. "I will never leave you, nor forsake you" (Joshua 1:5).

Thank you, Abba.

Amen.

2 Corinthians 4:16

Therefore we do not lose heart. Though outwardly we are wasting away, yet inwardly we are being renewed day by day.

Some days, I feel like I could run a marathon; other days, I feel like a *live* a marathon. Every day, though, Lord, the sun comes up and renews my hope. Today is a new day with new situations, new challenges, and new frustrations. Yet I will not lose heart, for you are with me at every twist and turn. You have prepared me for today in and out, up and down, beginning to end. I feel no worries, for you take care of those, Lord. Today is new, so my attitude is new. Here's to today.

Amen.

Lamentations 1:20

See, O Lord, how distressed I am! I am in torment with in, and in my heart I am disturbed, for I have been most rebellious. Outside, the sword bereaves; inside, there is only death.

Oh Lord, when I ran across this passage, deep in my heart, I hoped that perhaps the situation would not arise where I'd need it in writing a prayer. But history is repeating itself, so here I am in the same distressing situation that has happened again and again. This predicament is not new; outside the situation is _____ (fill in the blank).For me, it's a child. (It could be thousands of things. God wants to hear our troubles.) Inside the situation is _____ (fill in the blank for your situation).For me, I'm dealing with disappointment for the millionth time, it seems. Oh Lord, I don't want to be disappointed again. It hurts so much. Is there something I should be learning? Please forgive me for when I've been wrong. I've tried to do my best; it just seems to be not good enough. (Okay, maybe it is no coincidence that when I originally wrote this, it was April Fools' Day.) Is this a joke? No such luck. Father God, change my attitude toward this situation, both inside and out. Even though I am very sad and disappointed, make everything work out to your glory. Help me see the good that can come out of a seemingly bad situation.

I do not know what it's all about.

Change my heart inside and out.

Amen.

Psalm 4:4

In your anger do not sin, when you are on your beds, search your hearts, and be silent.

God, sometimes I feel like just crawling into bed, pulling up the covers, and hiding from everyone and everything. I need to go to a quiet place and do a little soul-searching right now. Sometimes I go for a walk, or sometimes my car is a nice, quiet place. As I look for words, the thing that is heavy on my heart is disappointment. Disappointment leads to anger, if I think about it. Father God, help me not to get angry—I may say something I'll regret. Tomorrow is a new day. As I learn from my yesterdays, today is all I have. Right now, I'm silently listening to my heavenly Father's voice.

Amen.

2 Chronicles 16:9

For the eyes of the Lord range throughout the earth to strengthen those whose hearts are fully committed to him.

Lord, you look for me. I picture a lighthouse on the shore warning ships of danger. I picture huge storm clouds parting to give way to the sun. I think of a headlight on a car. All these lights, while protective and beneficial, are finite; their range is finite. You, oh Lord, can see everyone everywhere. You are infinite. Thank you for keeping me in your sights, Lord.

Amen

Hebrews 3:7–8

So, as the Holy Spirit says, "Today if you hear his voice, do not harden your hearts."

Spirit of God, I hear you through every singing bird. I feel the warmth of the sun, and I smell the awakening earth. I am here, Lord, and I hear you. I am filled with peace because I know that my redeemer lives. I see an empty tomb, filled with the promise of my risen Savior. Hallelujah!

Amen.

Psalm 119:69–70

Though the arrogant have smeared me with lies, I keep your precepts with all my heart. Their hearts are callous and unfeeling, but I delight in your law.

Father God, I was hurt by lies today. Someone very dear to me became angry and made false accusations about me. Lord, I lift up this person to you in a very heartfelt prayer. I cling to your promises tightly now, Lord. You will never leave us nor forsake us. I may feel abandoned by this person, but Lord, you never abandon us. You are right here with me, and I pray that you are very near to the person who was angry with me. Father God, bring the three of us together to mend our relationship as only our heavenly Father can do.

Amen.

Psalm 4:7–8

You have filled my heart with greater joy that when their grain and new wine abound. I will lie down and sleep in peace, for you alone, O Lord, make me dwell in safety.

Lord, I will rejoice. From when I get up this morning to when my head hits the pillow tonight, I will keep but one word on my mind and in my heart: joy. Yes, joy. Father God, I thank you for the joy that fills me today.

A joy-filled amen.

Isaiah 26:8

Yes, Lord, walking in the way of your laws, we wait for you; your name and renown are the desire of our hearts.

Lord God, why is waiting so hard? I feel like I'm always waiting for someone or something. I like it when people are timely, but so much of what we wait for is out of our control. I can't move the hands of time any more than I can control the sun rising and setting. We try to explain all the miracles on earth with the laws of physics, logic, matter, inertia, and mass. But God, you set this earth spinning on its axis. These are your laws. You created them. I try to understand them, but I cannot. That's where faith comes in, doesn't it? I have complete faith in you, oh God. No matter what, my heart desires your plan.

Amen.

Colossians 3:23

Whatever you do, work at it with all your heart, as working for the Lord, not for men.

Lord God, this is the perfect passage for me. You have no idea. (Well, yes you do, because you're God.) Sometimes I wonder if I'm in the right job, profession, or place in life. I question this often. You, through this passage, assured me that I am. When I think about my work, it's not simply where I earn a paycheck. I try to do my best always, but the politics, personalities, and protocols weigh me down—way down. When I change my perspective and work with all of my heart (as if you were signing my paycheck), my attitude changes. Lord, you gave me certain gifts and abilities. You made me the right fit for what I am doing. I will do my very best work today, tomorrow, and always.

Amen.

Psalm 61:2

From the ends of the earth I call to you, I call as my heart grows faint; lead me to the rock that is higher than I.

Lord God, you are the rock that is higher, oh so much higher than I. From your vantage point and unlimited wisdom, you see the whole picture. I don't; I only see a part of the whole. I trust totally that from your vantage point, this situation is totally under control. Sometimes the world seems so out of control. I will focus only on you and your leading. When my heart grows faint, I look to you for guidance.

Amen.

Psalm 105:3

Glory in his holy name; let the hearts of those who seek the Lord rejoice.

Holy God, today, in itself, is an answered prayer. The sun came up this morning, filling me with hope. I can find you in the simple wonders that happen, turning any ordinary day into an extraordinary one. I rejoice in your presence throughout each day.

Amen.

Psalm 73:21

When my heart was grieved and my spirit embittered …

Father, my spirit feels very embittered today. I had a lot of stuff thrown at me from work and family. I felt like crying—I did, in fact. My prayer was, "Lord, what am I supposed to be learning from all this?" I have a choice here, don't I? I can be overwhelmed by it, orI can hand it all over to you and we can overcome it together. I choose the latter. Here you go:

Take this trouble; you're in control.

I only see part; you see the whole.

Amen.

Romans 8:27

And he who searches our hearts knows the mind of the Spirit because the Spirit intercedes for the saints in accordance with God's will.

Holy, Holy Spirit of God,

Search my heart with an all-knowing eye.

My human vision is tainted, no matter how hard I try.

May I be a blessing in whatever I do,

Remembering my gifts and talents all come from you.

Amen.

Job 7:17–18(NKJV)

What is a man, that you should exalt him, that you should set your heart upon him, that you should visit him every morning?

Yahweh, today I come to you in the beautiful morning. The sun is shining, the earth is awake, and so am I. Come near to me now;

let's sit together, Lord, and converse through prayer about whatever is on our hearts.

Amen.

2 Corinthians 4:1

Therefore since it is God's mercy that we are engages in this ministry we do not lose heart.

God, how do you want me to be a minister? Is it by writing? Is it by my profession? Is it in some sort of service? Do you want me to travel? How do I know if what I'm doing is correct? Wait. Let me back up a moment. I can't do everything, yet I do feel compelled to keep writing. The more I dig into Scripture and write these prayers, the more things become clearer. The Lord has me in the right place, doing the right thing in his perfect timing. To whoever's eyes are reading this prayer, I ask you this question, "What ministry is God asking you to be a part of? Ask, pray, and talk to God about it. Then listen, do, and be blessed in the response God gives you."

Amen.

Proverbs 19:21

Many are the plans of a man's heart, but it is the Lord's purpose that prevails.

Lord, I am a planner. I like organization. I like balance. That's just me. Help me not to make an idol of planning. My husband calls me his *little over-achiever.* I've been that way as long as I can remember. It has served me well. I always studied a lot and got good grades in school. I suppose that's all great, Lord, but help me not to be chained to my to-do list. Organize my day in accordance with your purpose, Jesus. Together we will accomplish whatever it is that is on our hearts.

Amen.

Psalm 86:11

Teach me your way, O Lord, and I will walk in your truth; give me an undivided heart, that I may fear your name.

Lord, help me stand firm. I know what is true: you are my Lord, my God, the one I trust. There is no other. As the world and all its issues swirl around me this way and that, I have beating in my chest an undivided heart—one that belongs to you alone.

Amen.

Hebrews 12:3

Consider him who endures such opposition from sinful men, so that you will not grow weary and lose heart.

Jesus, you endured so much. I wish I could see you and live when you lived, but that's not possible. I was born to live now and I'll see you in heaven. But until then, I'll keep going, keep plugging along. I will not lose heart. Quite to the contrary, this passage including Hebrews 12:2, encourages me into action. I will endure.

Amen.

2 Corinthians 4:16

Therefore we do not lose heart. Though outwardly we are wasting away, yet inwardly we are being renewed day by day.

Lord, I am in the middle of something. On the outside, it would seem like this is not going to ever come together in a good way. I am so overwhelmed that I want to put my face in my hands and cry, but that won't really solve anything. So I take a deep breath, and look outside. The sun came up and my day began. Renew, regenerate, refresh, and regroup. Renew, yes. Every day is a new day, a new opportunity for growth and challenge. Lose heart? No way. Lord, we make it, day by day.

Amen.

Joshua 2:11

When we heard it, our hearts melted and everyone's courage failed because of you, for the Lord your God is God of heaven above and on earth below.

God of heaven,

Situations happen—

Things we cannot explain.

"Why did God let this happen to me?" we ask.

The Israelites of the Old Testament goofed up.

The disciples goofed up.

I goof up.

Melt my human heart, oh God.

Help me to realize my short-comings.

You, oh God, are the God of heaven and earth.

Forgive me.

Help me learn.

Help me grow.

Amen.

Psalm 51:17

The sacrifices of God are a broken spirit, a broken and a contrite heart, O God, you will not despise.

Oh God, there are days I just feel broken. My body ages. Time marches on. Things are not made to last. They seem to break, get tossed aside, and forgotten. Yet you, oh God, do not toss us aside. We may feel useless, but that is specifically when you do your best work on us, Lord. We may feel broken, yet that's exactly when we are strong, because we lean on you. When we are down and out, the only way we have is up. Then we look heavenward, with humble hearts, and wait patiently.

Amen.

1 Peter 3:15

But in your hearts set apart Christ as Lord. Always be prepared to give an answer to everyone who asks you to give the reason for the hope that you have. But do this with gentleness and respect.

Dearest Jesus, I had the opportunity to witness to a new neighbor today, a family who just moved in. I asked if they had a church-home yet. I told them where I go to church and also told them of all the other churches in the area. That's all I did, Lord. I know in my heart you are truly set apart. I do not know what will come of our conversation, but you, Lord, can take it from here. I hope that I will have future conversations with my neighbors. Lord, may my words be chosen with kindness and respect. Bless all my neighbors.

Amen.

Hosea 7:14

They do not cry out to me from their hearts but wail on their beds. They gather together for grain and new wine but turn away from me.

If you wallow in your sorrow, then there's nothing good tomorrow.

If you pray in your today, then the Lord will have his say.

So tonight turn out the light, because it will be all right.

The carpenter from Nazareth will fix it.

(I thought of this while riding my bike.)

Lord, I don't want to wallow in my sorrow or lie on my bed feeling sorry for myself. When I'm feeling blue, help me to paint my attitude a different color. Self-pity is unattractive. You have made me unique—like no one else on earth. I praise you and thank you for this from my heart.

Amen.

Isaiah 29:13

The Lord says: "These people come near to me with their mouth and honor me with their lips, but their hearts are far from me. Their worship of me is made up only of rules taught by men."

Father God, say this is not so. I never want my heart to be far from you. I pray the words that come from my lips go first through the filter of my heart. My mind is full of many rules and tainted by propriety. We never want to offend anybody nowadays. Lord, I don't want to offend you. Help me speak the truth; always back up my words with your Word. Be near to me, Lord.

Amen.

1 Kings 8: 22–24

Then Solomon stood before the altar of the Lord in front of the whole assembly of Israel, spread out his hands toward heaven and said: "O Lord, God of Israel, there is no God like you in heaven above or on earth below---you who keep your covenant of love with your servants who continue wholeheartedly in your way. You have kept your promise to your servant David my father; with your mouth you have promised and with your hand you have fulfilled it---as it is today.

Not a portion or a part; no, Lord, my whole heart. My plans, dreams, past, present, and future—all that is me and who you created me to be—are wrapped up together in your covenant of love. You are the amazing God of heaven and earth. No one compares. You are above and below; no matter where I go, we face everything together.

Amen.

1 Kings 8:38–39

And when a prayer or plea is made by any of your people Israel---each one aware of the afflictions of his own heart, and spreading out his hands toward this temple---then hear from heaven, your dwelling place. Forgive and act; deal with each man according to all he does, since you know his heart (for you alone know the hearts of all men).

Father in heaven, you know what the affliction of my heart is right now. You know me so well. I treasure our relationship, Lord, for I can tell you everything. You know what my heart holds. Right now it holds worry, but I spread out my hands and I offer it all up. I let it go because I know you are hearing me right now from heaven.

Amen.

1 Kings 8:58

May he turn our hearts to him, to walk in his ways and to keep his commands, decrees and regulations he gave our fathers. And may these words of mine, which I have prayed before the Lord our God day and night, that he may uphold the cause of his servant and the cause of his people Israel according to each day's need.

Father, I do need to turn over my heart and my attitude. They've been negative lately. I must look at the positive. One little line changes a minus into a plus. One little added letter makes miles into smiles. May I be that positive little change today.

Amen.

1 Kings 8:61

But your hearts must be fully committed to the Lord our God, to live by his decrees and obey his commands, as at this time.

God, at this time, life is good. At this time, life is bad. Is the glass half full or is it empty? It's all about perspective. I choose the positive, not the negative. I make this commitment at this time and in your timing, Lord.

Amen.

2 Corinthians 1:9

Indeed, in our hearts we felt the sentence of death. But this happened that we might not rely on ourselves but on God, who raises the dead.

There are many days, Lord, when I do not feel like getting out of bed. I read the headlines, battle traffic, and work in a stressful job. I feel like all I'm doing is fighting one thing or another. Can I give up Lord?

No! It's not just about me. Lord, you have overcome all my worries and fears. I need not be afraid of anyone or anything, including death.

My heart is set on heaven. I'm just not in heaven—not yet, anyway. You have a job for me to do, and I'll rely on you.

Amen.

John 14:27

Peace I leave with you; my peace I give you. I do not give to you as the world gives. Do not let your hearts be troubled and do not be afraid.

Jesus, how did you know I needed this passage so very much? I'm going to read it again.

It's very timely with so much going on in my life that causes my eyes to fill with tears as I write these very words. Jesus, I picture you wiping away these tears rolling down my cheeks. Can I just bury my head in your shoulder and stay here wrapped in your peaceful presence for a while? "I'll give you as long as you need, because I'll never leave you or forsake you" (Hebrews 13:5). "Do not let your hearts be troubled, Trust in God and trust also in me" (John 14:1). I fully trust you with my troubled heart. Thank you, Jesus, for holding me close to you right now.

Amen.

Matthew 12:34

You brood of vipers, how can you who are evil say anything good? For out of the overflow of the heart the mouth speaks.

Help me at all times today.

Guard my mouth about what I say.

Let my voice come from my heart

Where you are present from the start.

Amen.

Proverbs 6:20–21

My son, keep your father's commands and do not forsake your mother's teaching. Bind them upon your heart forever; fasten them around your neck.

To be a parent is such a blessing. Lord, I thank you for my children and my parents. May I be a blessing to them, as they have been to me. May we not get on each other's nerves. May we have an air of understanding, mutual respect, and kindhearted love. May the memories that we have made in the past be shared with future generations of our family. Lord, bless us all with hope, joy, and love for each other today, tomorrow, and always.

Amen.

1 Corinthians 14:25

And the secrets of his heart will be laid bare. So he will worship God, exclaiming, "God is really among you!"

Lord, I don't want any secrets between us. You made me who I am. I confess all that I failed to do or did for the wrong reasons. Forgive me for when I spoke instead of listening, or judged when I should have offered a shoulder to lean on, or turned a blind eye when I perceived something to be wrong. Lord, may I worship you by my actions, may I glorify you with my words, and may I fall on my knees in prayer before making a move in any direction. Hear my prayer, Lord. It's from my heart.

Amen.

James 4:7–8

Submit yourselves, then, to God. Resist the devil, and he will flee from you. Come near to God and he will come near to you. Wash your hands, you sinners, and purify your hearts, you double-minded.

Remember

Even

Satan

Is

Silenced

Today

Why?

Because God is always near, and he's the only one I hear.

Amen.

Proverbs 19:21

Many are the plans of a man's heart, but it is the Lord's purpose that prevails.

Lord, I freely admit, I'm a planner and a list-maker. Whereas it's okay to be organized, help me to put my plans into your hands. I don't see the whole picture, but you do. My heart is calm because I have a clear purpose in view. I may not see what's over the horizon or beyond the next hill or valley, but that's all right. You are already there. With the wind of your Holy Spirit in my soul, filling my sails with the energy I need, it is your purpose for me that will prevail.

Amen.

Hebrews 8:10

This is the covenant I will make with the house of Israel, after that time, declares the Lord. I will put my laws in their minds and write them on their hearts. I will be their God and they will be my people.

God, you are a writer just like I am. Okay, maybe that's a stretch. Yet I have such a passion for sharing with people what you mean to me. I can do this by sharing in the prayers I write revealing how Scripture comes alive to me. When my pen meets paper, I am so inspired. To whoever is reading this, I ask," What has God written on your heart?" Just ask the Lord, and he will answer. From me to you, blessings on his answer to you.

Amen.

Luke 10:27

He answered: "Love the Lord your God with all your heart and with all your soul and with all your strength and with all your mind; and Love your neighbor as yourself."

Lord God, help me to love completely with mind, soul, strength, and heart. Head to toe, in and out, front to back, beginning to end. Your love never ends. My life is finite here on earth, but I will spend eternity in heaven with you, Lord. Your love never fails. I fail here on earth; I am imperfect. I make mistakes. Your love is strong. Help me to love with the might and strength that comes from you. Energize, uphold, and encourage me as I do for others what you do for me today, tomorrow, and always.

Amen.

Psalm 112:7

He will have no fear of bad news; his heart is steadfast, trusting in the Lord.

Good morning, Lord.

I am off to face the day. Fear is nowhere to be found in my heart's vocabulary because I am trusting you with each step I take. Faith moves my foot forward because there will be a place for my foot to land on, a stepping stone. A steadfast path is the one I take, trusting you, Lord, in the steps I make.

Amen.

Psalm 112:8

His heart is secure, he will have no fear; in the end he will look in triumph over his foes.

Good evening, Lord.

Jesus, it is the end of a long day. Good day? Bad day? Stressful day? Joyful day? Yes, for many reasons all of those words can be used to describe today. Lord Jesus, thank you for triumphantly getting me through it all. My heart can rest in the security of your love and faithfulness. Now I will close my eyes and sleep because no fear rests with me; for you, oh Lord, are my security blanket.

Amen.

Colossians 2:2–3

My purpose is that they may be encouraged in heart and united in love, so that they may have the full riches of complete understanding, in order that they may know the mystery of God, namely Christ, in whom are hidden all the treasures of wisdom and knowledge.

Lord, thank you for this verse. It is so upbeat. I picture you standing at the sidelines, cheering us on, encouraging our hearts. You know each step before we take it. Things are not always perfect. Life is what we make of it. So I offer up this prayerful, *Yahoo!* Lord. There's a smile in our hearts thanks to you.

Amen.

Genesis 8:21-22

The Lord smelled the pleasing aroma and said in his heart: "Never again will I curse the ground because of man, even though every inclination of his heart is evil from childhood. And never again will I destroy all living creatures, as I have done."

"As long as the earth endures, seed time and harvest, cold and heat, summer and winter, day and night will never cease."

God, I hear the news. The world seems to be filled with disasters: floods, earthquakes, war, famine, disease, and unrest. Don't you just look at us sometimes and want to disown us? But that's not your nature, is it, Lord? Just like you promised Noah, you won't destroy all living creatures. What can I offer up to you, Lord, as a promise from my heart to yours? Since I'm not going to really light a fire, as was the custom in Noah's time, I offer up instead this very prayer to you. May it float through the air to heaven, which I know to be a very real place.

May the angels lift their voices.

May all the saints sing along.

May heaven and earth all praise you,

For this is my prayerful song.

Amen.

1 Samuel 16:7

But the Lord said to Samuel, "Do not consider his appearance or his height, for I have rejected him. The Lord does not look at the things man looks at. Man looks at the outward appearance, but the Lord looks at his heart".

Lord, you have special X-ray vision, don't you? You see what my heart truly feels and thinks about, all of my motives, desires, hopes, and dreams. Nothing is hidden from you. This thought is comforting to me, as well as convicting. Diagnose issues and make them known to me, Lord, so that my heart is strong, vibrant, and beating in time with your will.

Amen.

Psalm 33:21

In him our hearts rejoice, for we trust his holy name.

Holy One, my heart truly rejoices this day. The storm came and went without damage. I see evidence that it was here: puddles and downed branches, but I also see vibrant green. Storms in life come and go.

Some create damage; others don't. No matter what happens, we trust the outcome rests securely in your hands. Just like you, Jesus, while on the stormy Sea of Galilee, I slept through the storm last night. This morning my heart rejoices in your creation.

Amen.

2 Chronicles 6:30

Then hear from heaven, your dwelling place. Forgive, and deal with each man according to his heart (for you alone know the hearts of men).

God in heaven,

You know my heart. You know what's inside.

I have nothing to fear. I have nothing to hide.

You forgive and you heal,

You listen to it all

When I succeed, but even more so when I fall.

Amen.

Job 22:21–22

Submit to God and be at peace with him; in this way prosperity will come to you. Accept instruction from his mouth and lay up his words in your heart.

God, why do I feel like I'm always running after goals: to achieve, to impress, and to get ahead? I could go on and on. This is not the way to acquire peace, is it, Lord? I need to accept instruction from you. Today, I heard someone say, "You don't have to be good at everything." Sometimes I feel like I'm pursuing my goals, and they are not in harmony with what your plan is for me. Achieving things and titles should not be my goal. I know in my heart that I should be at peace exactly where I am now. Thank you, God, for this wake-up word. True prosperity is not measured in money or fame.

True prosperity comes, not in a box with a bow.

It's finding peace, letting God, and letting go.

Amen.

Psalm 7:9

O righteous God, who searches minds and hearts, bring to an end the violence of the wicked and make the righteous secure.

Righteous God, all I have to do is open a paper or watch the news and it's everywhere. Violence in so many forms and throughout the globe seems to permeate our lives, regardless of income, race, creed, opinion, or religion. I tend to get caught up in the bad. Search my heart, Lord, and help me see the good, too.

1 John 4:16: God is love.

1 John 4:18: There is no fear in love.

1 John 4:19: We love him because he first loved us.

1 John 4:21: Whoever loves God must also love his brother.

I find security in your perfect love, oh God. I find my true security in you.

Amen.

Exodus 10:1

Then the Lord said to Moses, "Go to Pharaoh, for I have hardened his heart and the hearts of the officials so that I may perform these miraculous signs of mine among them."

Lord, people with hard hearts are often hardest to love. Help me see them through your eyes, for sometimes the people who make our lives most difficult are actually the ones you, Lord, work through.

Moses obeyed you, even though he was up against a wall—an insurmountable one. Today I pray for a heart that has fortitude and confidence so that, no matter what or who I encounter this day, I know you are at work among us.

Amen.

1 Chronicles 29:18

O Lord, God of our fathers Abraham, Isaac and Israel, keep this desire in the hearts of your people forever, and keep their hearts loyal to you.

Lord, you are the God who loves his children, grandchildren, great-grandchildren, and so on. You have loved us for generations and will continue to do so until time ends. Lord, help me to be a patient parent, just like you are. This is the desire of my heart.

Amen.

Psalm 17:10

They close up their callous hearts and their mouths speak with arrogance.

Holy Spirit, today I pray for a soft heart. Lately, I have felt that others have told me all about their successes. I have listened patiently, but secretly, my heart's full of jealously. You know my heart. I confess this sin to you. I am not proud of it. Holy One, cleanse and create within me a proper spirit. Infuse my heart with love and compassion for others. Take the *arrow* out of arrogance so that the words I use today put the *courage* into encouragement.

Amen.

Psalm 62:8

Trust in him at all times. O people; pour out your hearts to him, for God is our refuge.

Okay, Lord, I'm pouring it out—all out. Today was a disaster. The tears just kept coming. But exactly when I thought all was lost, wham! Answered prayer. What I perceived to be a disaster ended up not being one. I trust in you completely. I never doubted, really, I just wasn't sure how this would work. You are a timeless God, yet we are in a time–plagued world. Thank you for being in timely control, Lord.

Amen.

Proverbs 11:20

The Lord detests men of perverse heart but he delights in those whose ways are blameless.

Lord God, when I open the paper each day, I see perverse things. I guess that's what sells papers, but really? There are a lot of weird people out there, yet today I had a lady at the Pack-n-Mail go out of her way to help me locate a package. One of my coworkers was available just when I needed help, and today a dear friend retired from our place of employment after many years of dedicated service. Those are all good, awesome, admirable things. I want to focus on the good, and not the bad. Can you blame me, Lord? No way.

Amen.

Isaiah 29:13

The Lord says: "These people come near to me with their mouth and honor me with their lips, but their hearts are far from me. Their worship of me is made up only of rules taught by men."

Father God, there are so many rules: rules at work, rules of the road, rules of conduct, rules of games, and rules at school. Sometimes the rules even contradict each other. Yikes! I know we need rules to function as a society or we would crumble into chaos. God, you gave Israel the Ten Commandments in the Old Testament. These were not the rules made by men, but were given to Moses at Mount Sinai by you. You wrote them on tablets of stone so we could remember them. That seems like a very long time ago. Your Son, Jesus, added another commandment: "Love the Lord your God with all your heart and with all your soul and with all your mind and with all your strength."(Note Mark 12:30 in the next prayer.) Father, help me to remember your commandments by writing them on the tablet of my heart.

Amen.

Mark 12:28–31

One of the teachers of the law came and heard them debating. Noticing that Jesus had given them a good answer, he asked him, "Of all the commandments, which is the most important?" "The most important one, "answered Jesus, "is this: 'Hear O Israel, the Lord our God, the Lord is one. Love the Lord your God with all your heart and with all your soul and with all your mind and with all your strength.' The second is this: 'Love your neighbor as yourself.' There is no commandment greater than these."

Jesus, here are the additional commandments you gave to your Father's original ten. Between you and me, Jesus, I like yours better. Mind you, loving someone with all your heart, mind, soul, and strength, well, that's asking a lot, don't you think? Today, with all my heart and with your help, I will do my best.

Amen.

Mark 3:5

He (Jesus) looked around at them in anger and, deeply distresses at their stubborn hearts, said to the man, "Stretch out your hand." He stretched it out and his hand was completely restored.

Jesus, I wish you were right here, ready and able to heal. There is someone who is on my heart right now who could really use your healing touch. I don't have a stubborn heart, just a very concerned and distressed parent's heart. I don't like being so far away. I feel helpless. All I can do is pray right now. I can't fix the injury; that will take time to heal. Today I humbly pray for restoration. What you require is patience to mend and heal someone in pain.

Amen.

Romans 1:21

For although they knew God, they neither glorified him as God nor gave thanks to him, but their foolish hearts were darkened.

God, I never, ever want to forget to thank you for what you do for me each day. In fact, I am breathing, living, and enjoying your wonderful creation. This is reason enough to be thankful every minute. Never let my heart darken, separated from your marvelous light. Today is the longest day of the year, the summer solstice. I appreciate every minute of daylight. The summer breezes are fragrant and the evenings are long. What a glorious time of year summer is. I thank you for the flowers in my garden, the birds, and the frogs I hear croaking away in the slowly fading daylight. I thank you for this time of year. I thank you for summer. I thank you, Lord.

Amen.

Exodus 14:4

"And I will harden Pharaoh's heart, and he will pursue them. But I will gain glory for myself through Pharaoh and his army, and the Egyptians will know that I am the Lord." So the Israelites did this.

Father God, bad, even overwhelming things happen. The people I love get hurt. Sometimes it seems life is pursuing me and my family, like Pharaoh did the Israelites. Situations seem unfair and ruthless right now. How can you allow this? Yet, Lord, as you protected Israel from coldhearted Pharaoh, you also promise to protect us.

Deuteronomy 31:6 says, "Be strong and courageous. Do not be afraid or terrified, because of them for the Lord your God goes with you; he will never leave you or forsake you!"

May you, Lord, be glorified as you walk by our side.

Amen.

1 Samuel 12:20

"Do not be afraid," Samuel replied. "You have done all this evil, yet do not turn away from the Lord, but serve the Lord with all your heart."

Lord, yes, I've been wrong. You revealed something to me yesterday. I get jealous of others, not necessarily of their possessions, but of their abilities. They have gifts I don't have. I just reread the last sentence I wrote, and I sound like a three-year-old having a temper tantrum. Forgive me, Lord. Remind me that we all serve you in different and unique ways. I write, while others may sew, cook, analyze, fix, speak, build, record, heal, plant, sing, mentor, teach, research, organize, or plan. We all serve the Lord in various ways, but let's all do it with our entire heart, starting today.

Amen.

Job 17:11

My days have passed, my plans have shattered, and so are the desires of my heart.

Lord God, it has been a great day and a horrible day. A really good thing happened and a really not so good thing happened. My husband always says, "Things happen for a reason." But really? I need some continuity in my life: steadiness and level ground, Lord. Yes, this is what I pray for today. I'm not making plans, Lord; I am not telling you what to do. I'm spent. I'm tired and I feel shattered. I need this day to pass. Okay, now I'm done ranting and raving. Sorry,

Lord; forgive me. I just desire peace. I will rest in your presence and gather all my thoughts—the good, the bad, and the ugly. Somehow this will all make sense tomorrow. I let go of today and let God take it from here.

Amen.

Psalm 44:21

Would not God discover it, since he knows the secrets of the heart?

God, I'm glad you know all my secrets. I have a lot of thoughts rolling around in this head of mine all of the time. I tend to compare myself too much with others. But you know that already, don't you, Lord? Why do I do this? It serves no purpose. I am what you created me to be. I have strengths and weaknesses, just like everybody else. Forgive me for comparing. Help me to discover new ways to challenge myself and to set new goals. Here's my goal for today:_____.

Does it match what you had in mind, Lord?

Thy will be done.

Amen.

Proverbs 3:3

Let love and faithfulness never leave you; bind them around your neck, write them on the tablet of your heart.

Lord, I like the fact that my heart is a piece of paper. I love writing and the word I feel you are choosing for me today comes from this passage. It could be "love," "faithfulness," "never leave you," "bind them," "write them," or "heart." All are great words. I'll pick one to think about and praise you all day long.

Amen.

Proverbs 17:22

A cheerful heart is good medicine, but a crushed spirit dried up the bones.

Rx: UCANBHAPPY

Take one moment to pray every day.

Possible side effects: smiling, laughter, happiness, positive attitude

Physician's signature: God, your heavenly Father

Unlimited refills.

Psalm 9:1

I will praise you, O Lord; with all my heart; I will tell of all your wonders.

Lord, I really do have much to be thankful for:

Relationships and responsibilities,

Family and friends,

Home and health.

And that's just what I can name off the top of my head. I could get much more specific. I will take time to go over a thankfulness list in my heart right now. But most of all, thank you for listening to this prayer, Lord.

Amen.

Proverbs 16:9

In his heart a man plans his course, but the Lord determines his steps.

Make

A

Plan for me, Lord! Your **D**etours

Exits

Turns

Events

Round-a-bouts

Merge

In

Not

Enter   my   **S**

                                                        T

                                                                E

                                                                        P

                                                                                S

                                                Amen

Proverbs 16:5

The Lord detests all the proud of heart. Be sure of this: They will not go unpunished.

I am having trouble sleeping, Lord. Here I am at 4:00am wide awake. My brain is flooded with ideas, people, problems, my to-do-list, work, kids, the future, and the past. On and on it goes. Why do I think I can solve any of this now? Do I think I can handle this all on my own? My pride is getting in the way of my rest. I will hand all this stuff over to you, Lord, knowing that tomorrow is a new day, containing new challenges and new achievements. Even you, Lord, rested on the seventh day of creation. Tomorrow is in your hands, Lord, not mine.

Amen.

2 Corinthians 4:16–17

Therefore we do not lose heart. Though outwardly we are wasting away, yet inwardly we are being renewed day by day. For our light and momentary troubles are achieving for us an eternal glory that far outweighs them all.

Jesus, this passage could not have come at a better time. I did feel like I was losing heart. I was overwhelmed, but again, you came through with renewal. Outside, craziness surrounded me; inside, I was overwhelmed, but I relied on my favorite one-word prayer: help! Guess what? You heard me, you answered me, and I feel renewed. Thank you, Jesus.

Amen.

Lamentations 1:22

My groans are many and my heart is faint.

Lamentations 5:15

Joy is gone from our hearts; our dancing has turned to mourning.

Lamentations 5:17

Because of this our hearts are faint …

Lamentations 2:18

The hearts of the people cry out to the Lord …

There is a reason this book of the Bible is called Lamentations.

It is filled with sadness and crying; frankly it's depressing.

As I step back and read theses passages again, we have all been to this place of deep sadness.

We bring the sadness to our heavenly Father who knows our hearts.

We leave it all up to you, oh God.

I prayerfully take the next step.

I let my sadness go and I give it up to you, God.

You are here for me—every minute of every day.

I may need to go through this process over and over,

But you are here, oh God, listening to this prayer.

Amen

Matthew 5:8

Blessed are the pure in heart, for they will see God.

Jesus, I do want to see you. I wish I could have been there to hear this sermon you gave. I wish I could have seen the look on the faces of the people as you spoke. Did they clap when you were finished, or just ask for more healings and miracles? What would I have done? Well, I won't know until I speak with you in heaven, but I need to keep my heart pure while I'm here. This is not easy. So many idols flash in my vision: fame, power, possessions. This is all temporary stuff. Our place in heaven is sealed for us in eternity because of your death and resurrection. This is purely amazing. How simply marvelous. I praise you, Jesus, with all my heart.

Amen.

Matthew 12:40

For as Jonah was three days and three nights in the belly of a huge fish, so the Son of Man will be three nights in the heart of the earth.

Jesus, I can't imagine three days and three nights in the dark, confined, alone, but alive. Jonah was defiant. Jesus was obedient. Abandoned, rejected, discarded, the way seemed impossible. The outcome seemed unattainable. The heart of the earth seemed to be the victor, but the heart of my Jesus is the light of the world. Jesus overcame death, darkness, and despair and in those three days and three nights we gained freedom from sin, a future in heaven, and faith in the truth. In three days and three nights …

Jesus, I *can* imagine.

Amen.

Genesis 24:45

Before I finished praying in my heart, Rebekah came out, with her jar on her shoulder. She went down to the spring and drew water, and I said to her, "Give me a drink."

God of Abraham, Isaac, and Jacob, this story goes deep into Old Testament history. What it says to me is that before Abraham finished praying, he received an answer. Rebekah was to be the future wife of his son, Isaac. History, although old stuff in yellowed pages, is still significant because you are still God. You listened to Abraham's prayer and you listen to ours to this day. We may not get an instantaneous answer like we do when pressing the Send icon for an e-mail because you work in God time. You are not confined to time; you created it. You are God of the past, present, and future. The end of this book has not been written yet.

Amen.

1 John 3:21–22

Dear friends, if our hearts do not condemn us, we have confidence before God and receive from him anything we ask, because we obey his commands and do what pleases him.

Jesus, sometimes I have trouble with confidence. I shy away rather than hold my ground. I'd rather let somebody else win which overrides my chance of failure. I'd rather back down than be a leader. Lord, I don't think that's doing my best. I stand before you now asking boldly for you to help me take the next step. You are there for me, win or lose, pass or fail. I won't go anywhere if I don't take the first step. Show me the way. Show me the way.

Amen.

1 Chronicles 16:10–12

Glory in his holy name; let the hearts of those who seek the Lord rejoice. Look to the Lord and his strength; seek his face always. Remember the wonders he has done, his miracles, and the judgments he pronounced.

Holy God, I look forward to the day when I will see you face-to-face in heaven. My vision will be unclouded by disease; I will need no corrective lenses. I will see your face with perfect clarity. While I look forward to this moment, I will see you every day, Lord, in the smiling eyes of good friends, loving family, and even perfect strangers. I rejoice in the future, Lord; it looks bright.

Amen.

Psalm 9:1

I will praise you O Lord, with all my heart; I will tell of your wonders.

One of the many things I wonder about, Lord, is the essence of prayer itself. How do you hear it all? Prayers of praise, prayers of grief, prayers of sorrow, prayers of thanks, prayers for guidance, and prayers of pain; you hear them all. My little mind cannot fathom it, but I am thankful you can. Praise God!

Amen.

Ephesians 1:18

I pray also that the eyes of your heart may be enlightened in order that you may know the hope to which he has called you, the riches of his glorious inheritance in the saints ...

Jesus, the eyes of my heart see the hope of heaven. My friends and family who have gone before know this glorious inheritance you have waiting for all of us. Jesus, my brother, your footprints marked this earth. You understand us. You gave everything in your precious life on the cross for this fallen world. Knowing that the hope of heaven awaits me, I will have a spring in my step today.

Amen.

Ephesians 5:19

Speak to one another with psalms, hymns and spiritual songs. Sing and make music in your heart to the Lord.

May the melody I hum keep in time with the beat of my heart, and may the music in my heart be spoken from my lips as words that are pleasing and positive to the Lord. May they be audible to others as good music to their ears.

Amen.

Ephesians 6:5–6

Slaves, obey your earthly masters with respect and fear, and with sincerity of heart, just as you would obey Christ. Obey them not only to win their favor when their eye is on you, but like slaves of Christ, doing the will of God from your heart.

Jesus, help me to look at my earthly boss as if I were employed by you. Help me supervise others as you would have me be in charge.

Jesus, help me today to be sincere, fair, and respectful to all those I encounter in my place of employment.

Amen.

Colossians 4:8

I am sending him to you for the express purpose that you may know about our circumstances and that he may encourage your hearts.

Lord, help me to be a friend who encourages others today. I want to be positive; it is not always easy in a negative world. I want to be hopeful to the helpless, or maybe it's helpful to the hopeless. No matter, for I refuse to let circumstance weigh me down. I do not want to seem false or preachy. Lord, let my smiles be genuine and my laughter true because the hope in my heart was placed there by you.

Amen.

John 14:27

Peace I leave you, my peace I give you. I do not give to you as the world gives. Do not let your hearts be troubled and do not be afraid.

Jesus, how did you know I needed this passage so very much? I'm going to read it again, as it is very timely. There is so much going on in my life that causes my eyes to fill with tears as I write these words. Jesus, I picture you wiping away these tears rolling down my cheeks. Can I just bury my head in your shoulder and stay here, wrapped in your peaceful presence for a while?

"I'll give you as long as you need. I will never leave you nor forsake you" (Hebrews 13:5).

"Do not let you hearts be troubled. Trust in God and trust also in me" (John 14:1).

I fully trust you with my troubled heart. Thank you, Jesus, for holding me close to you right now.

Amen.

Matthew 12:34

You brood of vipers, how can you who are evil say anything good? For out of the overflow of the heart the mouth speaks.

Lord God,

Help me at all times today.

Guard my mouth in what I say.

Let my voice come from my heart

Where you are present from the start.

Amen.

Deuteronomy 8:5

Know then in your heart that as a man disciplines his son, so the Lord your God disciplines you.

Heavenly Father, as a parent we set boundaries for our kids. You do the same as our heavenly Father. You set boundaries, but we cross them, and there are consequences. You always love your kids, even if you don't like what they do, right? Well, sometimes I feel like a two-year-old having a temper tantrum, or a teenager in a hormonal huff. But Father, I am all grown up now. I shouldn't need discipline, should I? Whoa, listen to your willful child. Sorry, forgive me. I need you like I need air. I need limits and rules, and I need to follow them as best I can. The word disciple comes from the word discipline. Help me, your disciple, to thrive in the discipline of my faith.

Amen.

Nehemiah 2:2

So the king asked me, "Why does your face look so sad when you are not ill? This can be nothing but sadness of heart."

I am saddened by the recent turn of events, Lord.

Nehemiah 2:12

I set out during the night with a few men. I had not told anyone what my God had put in my heart to do for Jerusalem.

I talked to my friend whom God had put on my heart (that included you, Lord).

Nehemiah 4:6

So we rebuilt the wall till all of it reached half its height, for the people worked with all their might.

The answer involved commitment, hard work, and dedication.

Nehemiah 7:5

So my God put it into my heart to assemble the nobles, the officials and the common people for registration by families.

So I assembled all the resources I could, including friends and family.

Nehemiah 9:8

You found his heart faithful to you, and you made a covenant with him to give to his decedents …You have kept your promise because you are righteous.

Whether the end of the story is, *they lived happily ever after* or not, you answered my prayer, Lord, because you are faithful.

Amen.

Ephesians 4:18

They are darkened in their understanding and separated from the life of God because of the ignorance that is in them due to the hardening of their hearts.

God, I don't want to be in the dark. Not that I want to know it all, either. Lord God, only you know all things, and I, as a believer, can only handle so much. My brain feels overloaded sometimes, bored sometimes, and over-stimulated sometimes. Information flows to and from with a click of a button; faster and faster with every passing day there's a new electronic toy. Communication is instantaneous. Sentences are shortened. With a click a message is sent. But where did it go? Lord God, I need not press a single button to talk to you. You are right here. We can talk heart-to-heart in prayer, anywhere, anytime. Keep my heart soft, pliable, and receptive to your voice. I love talking personally with you every day. Thank you for this time, Lord, because I know I am (Ctrl)-S: saved.

Amen.

Psalm 51:17

The sacrifices of God are a broken spirit; a broken and a contrite heart, O God, you will not despise.

Oh God, when someone leaves, I cannot help but be sad. Lord, I pray for their safety and well-being, but physically they are not with me. I know we are not here physically forever, but my heart is broken. I am very sad right now. But you are the God of heaven and earth. I know you have my loved one safely in your care. They may be a world and many time zones away, but you, oh God, are right there with them. My wish is for three things: a safe journey, encountering helpful people, and your company right along side them. I ask this sincerely, Lord, with all my heart.

Amen.

Mark 11:22–23

"Have faith in God," Jesus answered. "I tell you the truth, if anyone says to this mountain, Go, throw yourself into the sea and does not doubt in his heart but believes that what he says will happen, it will be done for him."

Jesus, I am opening up my heart to you because it contains sadness today. The tears are coming from loss and worry. Jesus, I believe that you alone can take my concerns away. I'm picturing myself physically handing them over to you, Jesus. I've heard it said by Margret Shepard, "Sometimes your only available transportation is a leap of faith." Oh, Jesus, I'm leaping because there is no shadow of a doubt that you will catch me.

D

O

N

E

Amen.

Ecclesiastes 2:10–11

I denied myself nothing my eyes desired; I refused my heart no pleasure. My heart took delight in all my work, and this was the reward for my labor. Yet when I surveyed all that my hands had done and what I had toiled to achieve, everything was meaningless, a chasing after the wind, nothing was gained under the sun.

Lord God, I ask for proper motivation, that my heart be in the right place and I do things for the right reasons. Sure, it's good to have goals, but are those goals in line with what your plan is? Lord, I need to slow down and survey what is important. Family and friends are so much more valuable than possessions and achievements. Help me never to lose sight of this.

Amen.

Ecclesiastes 2:20

So my heart began to despair over all my toilsome labor under the sun.

Do

I

Say

Poor me,

Another problem—

Impossible,

Rejected.　　**or**

Do

I

Stay

Positive

And

Invite

Restoration?

The choice is mine, Lord. I choose the second one.

Amen.

Ecclesiastes 5:2

Do not be quick with your mouth, do not be hasty in your heart to utter anything before God. God is in heaven and you are on earth, so let your words be few.

God, help me to hold my tongue. Even though I love to talk, help me, Father, not to let useless words fill the silence because I am uncomfortable with it. I need to be a listener and really listen.

Amen.

Ecclesiastes 5:20

He seldom reflects on the days of his life, because God keeps him occupied with gladness of heart.

I have a plaque in my kitchen that says:

Sorrow looks back,

Worry looks around,

Faith looks ahead.

My son said to me, "Mom, I think the last one should be *hope* instead of *faith*. So I took a piece of paper and wrote the word *hope* on it and covered up the word *faith* on the plaque.

Faith

Hope

To me hope is the "gladness of heart" for what lies ahead. I definitely have faith, too. I have faith that the Lord will take care of my family and friends. The words faith and hope are in this case interchangeable. Lord God, help my thoughts to be occupied with what is ahead today with gladness in my heart.

Amen.

Ecclesiastes 7:21–22

Do not pay attention to every word people say, or you may hear your servant cursing you---for you know in your heart that many times you yourself have cursed others.

God in heaven,

Words can

Build up,

Hurt,

Encourage,

Heal,

Mock,

Joke,

Make someone laugh,

Make someone cry.

Sometimes the same words, spoken in different tones, can mean all these things at once.

God, help me develop a tougher skin to protect a heart full of compassion.

Amen.

Ecclesiastes 8:5

Whoever obeys his command will come to no harm, and the wise heart will know the proper time and procedure.

Lord, wisdom is so much more than being book smart or getting A's on tests. Right now, my heart is very heavy. I feel weighted down by everything that happened today. Frankly, I was made to feel stupid, even though I did what I could, but so much was out of my control. So, you know what, Lord? The proper time is now. Now I am putting my day to bed; it's done, no more, time's up. Tomorrow is a new day. As the sun rises, so will my mood and outlook.

Amen.

Ecclesiastes 9:7

Go eat your food with gladness and drink your wine with a joyful heart, for it is now that God favors what you do.

God, I made a decision today. I prayed about it first, though. I heard your answer through others. You did not force my hand. I pray, Lord, that you find favor in this decision. This is not the easy way out, Lord. I'm headed into a challenging situation, and I know you'll be right by my side. I pray that you, Lord, find favor in what I do. I am taking a risk that is not easy for me. Lord, when I look at this situation I feel joy in my heart. I have no fear of the future, for you are on my side and at my side. Thank you, Lord.

Amen.

Ecclesiastes 10:2

The heart of the wise man inclines to the right, but the heart of the fool to the left.

Lord, I don't really understand this passage. I fully admit that. I'm going to take it to mean that I should be inclined to do what is right; I should follow the right path in life. Sometimes this is difficult. Life has so many twists and turns. I guess that's why, when we are at a crossroad or have a decision to make, we should simply get on our knees. Well, I'm on my knees. What's right, Lord?

Amen.

Ecclesiastes 11:9–10

Be happy, young man, while you are young, and let you heart give you joy in the days of your youth. Follow the ways of your heart and whatever your eyes see, but know that for all these things God will bring you judgment. So then, banish anxiety from your heart and cast off the troubles of your body, for youth and vigor are meaningless.

Lord, I really like this passage. It says three things about my heart: let your heart give you joy, follow the ways of your heart, and banish anxiety from your heart. The wisdom of this Scripture is timeless and ageless. We are all aging, but I have no fear of this fact. The wisdom I learn as I go through life I can pass on to my children and grandchildren. My youth is past, but I pray that you, oh Lord, will help me keep my heart young.

Amen.

2 Peter 1:19

And we have the word of the prophets made more certain, and you will do well to pay attention to it, as to a light shining in a dark place, until the day dawns and the morning star rises in your hearts.

Holy Spirit of God, just as the sun rises every day, please shine the light of your love in my heart today. May there be no darkness, no secrets, nothing hidden, and no place where the Sonshine of God does not penetrate.

Amen.

Psalm 4:6–8

Many are asking, "Who can show us any good?" Let the light of your face shine upon us O Lord. You have filled my heart with greater joy than when their grain and new wine abound. I will lie down and sleep in peace, for you alone, O Lord, make me dwell in safety.

Oh Lord, I do not think I can improve in any way David's prayer because you have filled my heart with so very much joy today. The future looks bright, especially when I look into the Sonshine of your love. As the sun sets on today, I rest in the knowledge that your love protects me as I sleep and continues on through whatever comes my way tomorrow. My heart is at peace.

Amen.

Psalm 9:1

I will praise you, O Lord, with all my heart, I will tell of your wonders.

Days, months, or even years from now, I will look back on my life and see how your loving guidance has made a path for my steps. I may try to wander now and again, but you, Lord, will hang in there with me through good times and bad, sunshine or storms. You never, ever let go of me. I praise you, oh Lord, with my words of praise through prayer.

Amen.

Deuteronomy 4:29

But if from there you seek the Lord your God, you will find him if you look for him with all your heart and with all your soul.

Lord, I love how you use your Word to speak. The words that jump from this passage are "from there." "There" is anywhere. I can call out to you from there anytime, anyplace, and you hear me. I look for your guidance today, Lord, and I praise your holy name from where I am right now. Your plan for me is good, but not necessarily easy.

Amen.

1 Corinthians 14:25

And the secrets of his heart will be laid bare. So he will fall down and worship God, exclaiming, "God is really among you!"

Friends don't keep secrets from one another. I'm horrible at keeping secrets; my conscience bothers me too much. Jesus, you are my friend and you did walk among us long ago. Today I can be your hands and feet and see you in the faces of those I encounter. Lord, I truly open my heart to you. You see what's inside; you see all my hopes, worries, fears, and dreams. Help me to be a true friend to others like you are to me.

Amen.

Psalm 86:11

Teach me your way, O Lord, and I will walk in your truth; give me an undivided heart, that I may fear your name.

Oh Lord, I'm not very good at making decisions quickly. I need to weigh the pros and cons, the positives and the negatives, and then I write out a side-by-side list. Finally, I make my choice. I don't experience remorse because I feel I have made my decision wisely and to the best of my ability. Everybody is different, however; you, Lord, made us all unique. When it comes to my faith, I am undivided. I do not waver, for my heart and soul remain securely devoted to the Lord above who loves me totally with his undivided heart.

Amen.

Proverbs 17:22

A cheerful heart is good medicine, but a crushed spirit dries up the bones.

Sometimes it's really hard to smile when things aren't going right.

We look so glum and teary-eyed and feel like giving up the fight.

A word of prayer is all it takes to turn it all around.

Help Lord, mouthed in a whisper, brings heaven's attention without a sound.

A smile or hug or handshake is what it takes to impart

A smile to someone's day—one that begins in your own cheerful heart.

Amen.

Romans 9:2

I have great sorrow and unceasing anguish in my heart.

Anything

Not of

God

Unnecessarily

Increases

Sadness and

Hardship.

Give it to God.

Open your heart.

Do accordingly.

Amen.

Ecclesiastes 5:2

Do not be quick with your mouth, do not be hasty in your heart to utter anything before God. God is in heaven and you are on earth, so let your words be few.

God in heaven, I love to write. As I write down these prayers, I pray continually for the people who read them. I pray that I glorify you with every one of these prayers. I pray for concise thoughts and clear ideas. This is important because prayer brings us close to you, Lord. You listen to each and every word. It is your Word (the Bible) that is the basis for what I write, the power behind the prayer, and the motivation in my heart.

Amen.

Exodus 7:13

Yet Pharaoh's heart became hard and he would not listen to them, just as the Lord had said.

What you say happens.

You speak only truth.

Father God, you speak and it comes true.

Help me to have a soft, pliable, listening heart,

One that is receptive to your spirit.

I don't ever want a hard heart like Pharaoh's,

One that is greedy, unyielding, and fickle.

Help me to listen before I speak

Only scriptural truth and trust in that truth.

Amen.

Exodus 7:14

Then the Lord said to Moses, "Pharaoh's heart is unyielding; he refuses to let the people go."

Lord, may there always be a yield sign in my heart. Help me to yield when I see a need. Help me to yield to your will. Yet, Lord, I pray for wisdom to discern when to not yield. Help me stand firm in my faith and not yield to my own or the world's selfishness. I guess that what I'm really praying for lies in the first part of this passage: "Then the Lord said to Moses …" Oh, how I wish I could hear your voice just like he did. I'm going to put my name in this passage instead of Moses' name. Then the Lord said to _____ (your name), and let my heart and ears yield to your response.

Amen.

Proverbs 4:20–22

My son, pay attention to what I say; listen closely to my words. Do not let them out of your sight, keep them within your heart; for they are life to those who find them and health to a man's whole body.

Pay attention, Lord? Is that what you're saying to me? I can't hear you. Wait, I'll turn off my cell, turn down the radio, and the TV. Kids, 'Can you shut the door?' Wait, my beeper's going off. Stop, stop,

Stop! Okay, I'm going into a room alone and shutting the door. There! Lord, I'm sorry, but now that the noise is gone, I can hear you. Let's just sit here together. I love these three verses from Proverbs.

Verse 20 says, "Listen to my words."

Verse 21 says, "Keep them within your heart."

Verse 22 says, "For they are life …and health to the body."

There's far too much to listen to out there, Lord.

Help me to hear your voice above and beyond the clatter.

For in your Word alone I will find what really matters.

Amen.

Psalm 147:3

He heals the broken hearted and bind up their wounds.

Lord, you're the Great Physician, healer, and listener. I picture you laying your hands on the untouchables when you were here on earth, and you continue to do the same from heaven. You provide me with friends and family who listen and give support, as I do for them. Sometimes, Lord, I feel helpless, for I do not know how to fix everybody's troubles, nor am I qualified or empowered to do so. Only you can do that, Lord. Help me today to be a good listener, without judgments or opinions. Help me to love and heal through my listening.

Amen.

Ephesians 3:17–18

So that Christ may dwell in your hearts through faith. And I pray that you, being rooted and established in love, may have power, together with all the saints, to grasp how wide and long and high and deep is the love of Christ.

This is how

High

Long ✝ wide

Deep

This is the love of Jesus Christ for us.

The cross, yes, that's it.

Your love is so wide, you're on my side.

Your love is so deep, it protects me when I sleep.

Your love is so long, it teaches me right from wrong.

Your love is so high, that when I die,

To heaven I'll go; all the saints will be there.

For now, though, I'll praise you through prayer.

Amen.

Psalm 101:2

I will be careful to lead a blameless life—when will you come to me? I will walk in my house with blameless heart.

Father, if you were a guest in my house, what would you hear? What would you see? Would I be proud of what was spoken? May the inside of my home match the outside. May guests be welcome and may peace greet you at the threshold.

Amen.

Proverbs 2:10

For wisdom will enter your heart, and knowledge will be pleasant to your soul.

Lord, I started something new, a new challenge. It's always a little scary, but I'm a better person for taking this risk. The more I get comfortable with my new environment, the more I will enjoy it. Sure, some days won't be the best, but that's okay for you, Lord, have the complete plan, and it's a good plan. It's you and me facing this day. I can only handle one day at a time. Help me not to look too far into the future, for although each day brings challenges, challenges can bring wisdom.

Amen.

Psalm 101:4

Men of perverse heart shall be far from me; I will have nothing to do with evil.

Lord, I cannot examine what a person's true motivations are or what's in their heart. Only you can, oh God. I am with people at work, or in line at the grocery store, or stuck in traffic. I am with people all day. Sometimes I just need to be alone. I need to recharge. Lord, tonight I pray for energy, not to be used right now, but for tomorrow! I will face tomorrow head-on because I know you are with me. Protect me from danger, but recharge me with your Spirit for whatever lies ahead.

Amen.

2 Corinthians 4:16

Therefore we do not lose heart. Though outwardly we are wasting away, yet inwardly we are being renewed day by day.

Yep, this ol' body just ain't what it used to be; neither is the brain. The world seems to be moving so fast with new technology, updates, and downloads. It all seems to be leaving me in the dust. Wait a minute. Day by day, minute by minute, you are with me, Lord. You don't leave me; you renew my strength to get up, face life, and keep learning. Every day is a gift, a gift to be renewed and to learn something new. My heart is not lost; it's found by being renewed in you.

Amen.

Ephesians 1:18

I pray also that the eyes of your heart may be enlightened in order that you may know the hope to which he has called you, the riches of his glorious inheritance in the saints.

Lord, sometimes aging, disease, emotions, preconceived ideas, and past experiences can all affect how I perceive situations. They can cloud my judgment. Today, shine your light into my day, onto the situations I encounter, and on the people I meet. Instill hope in my heart so that I see the potential that you see in people (that includes me). You have called me to be positive. May I pay it forward because it's what you called me to do.

Amen.

John 16:33

I have told you these things so that in me you may have peace. In this world you will have trouble. But take heart! I have overcome the world.

Thank you, Lord, for this passage.

You have overcome the world, but I still live here.

We do not live in what I would call a peaceful society.

Things seem to come at us from all angles—advertising, media, and entertainment.

Peace? What's that?

Lord, I want to be a student of peace.

I am taking baby steps in my training.

At times, an infant needs to be cradled in the arms of a loving parent.

Then there's the letting go of my parent's hand as I take my first steps.

Sure, I'll fall, but how else will I learn?

Help me to overcome the fears and failures of this life with faith

So that I may experience the peace you promise.

Fear→tension→pain—break the cycle.

Faith→take heart→talk to the Lord, peace.

Amen.

Psalm 26:2–3

Test me, O Lord, and try me, examine my heart and my mind; for your love is ever before me, and I will walk continually in your truth.

"Your love is ever before me." Thank you for that love. Lord, no matter what happens, your love surrounds me. Today I am not paying attention to *should you, could you, or would you* that I hear all around me. I want to heed only what my heavenly Father says in my heart.

Amen.

Isaiah 40:11

He tends his flock like a shepherd: He gathers the lambs in his arms and carries them close to his heart; he gently leads those that have young.

Heavenly Father,

Hold me close.

Hold my children close.

Hold my parents close.

This is a prayer for all generations.

We were all children once, no matter what our age.

I'm picturing you holding my family and me in a hug of prayer.

I just want to rest in this thought right now,

Snuggled on your shoulder, listening, heavenly Father, to your heart.

Amen.

Colossians 2:2

My purpose is that they may be encouraged in heart and united in love, so that they may have the riches of complete understanding, in order that they may know the mystery of God, namely, Christ.

You make it all work out, Lord.

I don't understand how, but you get it done.

Help me to stand up when someone who's down needs my chair.

Help me to stand back when my will gets in the way of yours, Lord.

Yet help me to understand that taking a stand is okay

As long as I'm standing firmly united by my faith in God

And in my Savior, Jesus the Christ.

Amen.

Genesis 6:5–6

The Lord saw how great man's wickedness on the earth had become, and that every inclination of the thoughts of his heart was only evil all the time. The Lord was grieved that he had made man on earth, and his heart was full of pain.

The last thing I ever want to do is grieve you, Lord, but I've got to say, there's something I've been thinking about. I hate taking risks; I like playing it safe, very safe. I feel that by doing so, I'll have this great, ordered life. But my quest for order is really a form of unbelief. I'm not trusting in your path for me. The inclination of my heart is safety and security. What is the inclination of your heart, Lord? I need to face my fears with faith instead of always playing it safe. Forgive me, Lord.

Amen.

Genesis 24:45

Before I finished praying in my heart, Rebekah came out, with her jar on her shoulder. She went down to the spring and drew water, and I said to her, "Please give me a drink."

God, you know what's in my heart. You know what I need before I ask. You know everything about me. Please, Lord, I'm praying for something. It might seem silly, but not to you. I'm praying in my heart. Listen.

Amen.

Deuteronomy 26:16

The Lord your God commands you this day to follow these decrees and laws; carefully observe them with all your heart and with all your soul.

We live in a world of rules. Some are good, some are bad, some are necessary, and some are unnecessary. I am not here to judge, but I am generally a rule-follower. Lord, my heart belongs to you. Keep it safely nears yours.

Amen.

Deuteronomy 28:65

Among the nations you will find no repose, no resting place for the sole of your foot. There the Lord will give you an anxious mind, eyes weary with longing, and despairing heart.

No rest,

Anxious mind,

Weary eyes,

Despairing heart.

This does not sound like a good place to be,

Yet it is where I am right now.

I feel so sad;

My heart's grieving.

Grieving takes time.

Help me grieve, Lord.

Tears come when I least expect them.

Mind, anxious,

Eyes, weary,

Heart, despairing,

Suppose I face this?

I'm turning my face to the sun, to the Son,

Son of God, Jesus,

My Savior—

The resting place for my soul.

Amen.

Deuteronomy 32:46

He said to them, "Take to heart all the words I have solemnly declared to you this day, so that you may command your children to obey carefully all the words of this law."

Lord, when Moses talked, people listened. Why don't my kids listen to me that way? Obey the words of the law? I pray my kids obey the words of the law. I pray for them right now. Father, like Moses prayed for the children of Israel, I pray for my children. Protect them, guide them, and guard them. Ground them. They are my children, but they are also your children, and so am I. I pray for all parents and children, heavenly Father, my Father.

Amen.

Joshua 22:5

But be careful to keep the commandment and the law that Moses the servant of the Lord gave you: to love the Lord your God, to walk in all his ways, to obey his commandments, to hold hast to him and to serve him with all your heart and all your soul.

Lord, your commandments are active, not passive. They teach us to love the Lord, walk in his ways, obey his commands, hold fast, and serve him. I cannot follow the commandments just by sitting there doing nothing. Lord, I'm motivated to be active; help me to stay in motion today.

Amen.

1 Samuel 12:20

"Do not be afraid," Samuel replied. "You have done all this evil; yet do not turn away from the Lord, but serve the Lord with all your heart."

Lord, your decrees are there to protect me, not to keep me in a cage. You put up a fence to keep me safe. On the inside, I'm free to serve you as I wish. I can choose to go over, under, or through the fence of your laws. But that's my choice and it's a risk. I can't do this on my own. You know best Lord. Please place honest people in my path who also serve you, to keep me honest and on track as Samuel did in this Scripture.

1 Samuel 12:24

But be sure to fear the Lord and serve him faithfully with all your heart; consider the great things he has done for you.

Lord, I can name a great thing you did for me today. You took a hopeless situation and made it hopeful. You took a bleak situation and made it bright. When today started, life looked glum, but dutifully, I placed one foot in front of the other. You had me encounter wonderful, caring people who helped me. Lord, this whole day you worked in and through others, and I did not realize it at the time. You are sovereign. As I consider this, only one phrase comes to mind: thank you.

Amen.

Psalm 14:1

The fool says in his heart, "There is no God." They are corrupt, their deeds are vile; there is no one who does good.

How can there be no God?

Look around.

Look at the sun, moon, stars, children, flowers, and your own hand.

Tell me there is no God?

God's hands made all this.

God made you, and we are all amazing creations

Who can praise and thank our creator.

I praise you for making us, God.

Amen.

Psalm 15:2

He whose walk is blameless and who does what is righteous, who speaks the truth from his heart …

Lord, I fully admit I make mistakes. I want to do what is right. Beating myself up does nothing. Learning from errors is the key. I need to speak the truth, do what is right, and in my heart, know that I am loved.

Amen.

Psalm 16:7

I will praise the Lord, who counsels me; even at night my heart instructs me.

"Now I lay me down to sleep. I pray the Lord my soul to keep."

A children's prayer, yet I'm all grown up now, Lord.

My prayer does not change.

Keep my home and family and friends safe.

The person who specifically comes to mind is_____.

This person is very close to my heart.

Lord, keep them close to your heart.

Amen.

Psalm 17:3

Though you probe my heart and examine me at night, though you test me, you will find nothing; I have resolved that my mouth will not sin.

Lord, sometimes my mouth can get me into trouble. Help me to think before I talk, and listen to the question before I give an answer. Help me to really hear what is spoken, quietly contemplate it, and then act according to what you speak in my heart.

Amen.

Psalm 18:45

They all lose heart; and come trembling from their strongholds.

Lord, today I do feel like I'm trembling. I can't put my finger on exactly why. Anger? Sadness? Depression? Maybe it's all of them. What is my stronghold? What do I have to let go of to be free to let you do your work in this situation? Lord, I just put aside my pride. I need you. Hold me, because I'm holding on to you.

Amen.

Psalm 19:8

The precepts of the Lord are right, giving joy to the heart. The commands of the Lord are radiant, giving light to the eyes.

Seeing light streaming in a window, no matter where it is, is a refreshing sight, for the sun has risen on a new day.

Sure, there may be challenges or bumps in the road, but, Lord, you give light to every situation.

You help me see the path that is ever before me; you give light to my eyes and joy to my heart.

No sunglasses needed, for the light is from heaven; the Son is the radiant One.

Amen.

Psalm 22:14

I am poured out like water, and all my bones are out of joint. My heart has turned to wax; it has melted away within me.

Lord, I recently had my heart melt. I saw someone begging on the street. She was holding a child and another child sat next to her. When did things get to this point? Where's the father of this family? My heart is filled with compassion for them, but as I reach in my pocket to give them money, I notice another person in need farther down the street. When does it end? How do we fix it? Well,

I prayed a blessing from Matthew 5:8: "Blessed are the poor in heart for they will see God." God blesses those who are poor and realize their need for him, for the kingdom of heaven is theirs. Jesus, you cared for the poor, needy, and desolate. By just touching them or speaking a word, those people were healed. You gave them hope. May the wax of my heart melt with compassion, but burn with the light of your hope. May I pray a prayer that does not judge; instead, may it bring joy.

Amen.

Psalm 25:17

The troubles of my heart have multiplied; free me from my anguish.

The troubles of my heart are multiplied.

This is how I see it.

My math:

Troubles X worry =emptiness.

God's math:

Find **R**est; **E**xperience **E**ternity.

My math is so short-sighted.

Lord, faith in you frees me from the present, empty situation,

And reminds me that my heart rests with you in heaven.

Amen.

Psalm 27:3

Though an army besiege me, my heart will not fear; though war break out against me, even then will I be confident.

Lord, on many days, life is a war zone. Watching the news, it seems like fear is knocking against the door—knocking, knocking, knocking. But wait, I don't need to let that fear enter. Why? Because I am confident of your love for me. I am armed with the weapon of your Word, confident in your control, and fearless in my faith.

Amen.

Psalm 30:12

That my heart may sing to you and not be silent. O Lord, my God, I will give you my thanks forever.

Oh Lord, I do have so very much to be thankful for. Yesterday, things seemed pretty glum, but things are looking up today. How about tomorrow? Who knows? It's not here yet. I actually caught myself humming and singing to myself. I was happy and am happy. It has been a long winter, but spring will arrive. (I bought some flower seeds; seeds give me hope.) And I will consciously try to pay it forward, for tomorrow I will carry a song in my heart, a purpose in my step, and a positive word on my lips.

Amen.

Psalm 32:11

Rejoice in the Lord and be glad, you righteous; sing all you who are upright in heart!

I do rejoice.

I have so much for which to be thankful.

I have so much to be glad about.

I have family and friends (such as they are).

I have today (such as it is).

I have my health (such as it is).

I have happiness.

I am glad because I have you, Lord.

Such a reason to rejoice!

Amen.

Psalm 36:10

Continue your love to those who know you, your righteousness to those who know you.

Father God, your love is continuous, forever, infinite, boundless. As I look left and right, up and down, forward and backward at my past, present, and future, I am so very thankful that I know you, Father.

Amen.

Psalm 38:8

I am feeble and utterly crushed; I groan in anguish of heart.

Could I cry any more tears?

Just when I am feeling better,

Wham!

Something makes me remember,

Like being hit with a two-by-four.

Lord, couldn't you warn me next time

So I could duck?

Hit again with grief, pain, and despair;

It's relentless.

But you know what, Lord?

Things got better after I just sat in silence.

No electronics, no phone or pager—

Nothing.

You and I calmly sat and listened to our

Beating hearts.

Amen.

Romans 15: 4–6

For everything that was written in the past was written to teach us, so that through endurance and the encouragement of the Scriptures we may have hope. May the God who gives endurance and encouragement give you a spirit of unity among yourselves as you follow Christ Jesus, so that with one heart and mouth you may glorify the God and Father of our Lord Jesus Christ.

Lord, I use your Word to write prayers. I love how at different times, different words hop off the pages of Scripture and I feel compelled to write prayers about these precious passages. I am so encouraged by these words in Romans. Sometimes I wonder if I am writing up to your heavenly standards. As I step back and read the last sentence I just wrote, I think about why I am writing this book of prayers in the first place. I feel compelled to tell people who you are, Lord. You are the God of the universe, and yet you listen to each and every prayer. You are amazing and I praise you for that. It is my hope that those who are reading this right now may be one with God's heart, because his heart loves them so much that he sent his son, Jesus Christ, to die on the cross.Blessings to them, for they are my friends in our Lord Jesus Christ.

Amen

Psalm 38:10

My heart pounds, my strength fails me; even the light has gone from my eyes.

Lord, why is it that I seem to react with panic at every turn, bump in the road, or change in plans? I don't want this shot of adrenalin to pierce my body all the time. Why does life have to be this way? Life is stressful, yet I need to react differently. I'm not acting in faith. I'd like to see the plans you have, but I can't. Today, Lord I pray for a piece of peace, so I can handle the challenges ahead. Thank you, Jesus.

Amen.

2 Peter 1:19

And we have the words of the prophets made more certain, and you will do well to pay attention to it, as to a light shining in a dark place, until the day dawns and the morning star rises in your hearts.

I love looking at the stars you created, Lord. And the flowers, oh they are beautiful. The smell of a baby, a kiss, the taste of ice cream, sand between my toes, wet grass in the morning dew, rainbows, fireflies, hummingbirds, miracles, miracles, miracles. They surround me, Lord. I breathe everything in and utter the words, "Thank you to the CEO. No, the COE: **C**reator **O**f **E**verything.

Amen.

Psalm 119:32

I run in the path of your commands, for you have set my heart free.

Freedom.

What does that mean to me, Lord?

I am free because I am forgiven.

I am free to make choices.

I have a free will.

Salvation is mine because of Jesus' sacrifice on the cross.

I choose Jesus.

He sets my heart free.

Freedom.

Amen.

2 Chronicles 16:9a

For the eyes of the Lord range throughout the earth to strengthen those whose hearts are fully committed to him.

Lord, I am totally committed to you. I see the amazing ways you work in situations every day. I pray today for strength to stand up for what's right, strength to speak up when necessary, and strength to hold back my words when I need to just listen. Finally, I pray for strength in my heart to discern the difference between these choices.

Amen.

Romans 2:5

But because of your stubbornness and your unrepentant heart, you are storing up wrath against yourself for the day of God's wrath, when his righteous judgment will be revealed.

Lord, is there a difference between stubbornness and persistence? I have trouble with change. Yes, I admit that I am resistant to it. The world moves so fast. It's hard to keep up. I feel left behind. I suppose every generation feels this way at some point. Forgive me, Lord. Turn my resistance into persistence.

Amen.

Luke 24:25

He said to them, 'How foolish you are, and how slow of heart to believe all that the prophets have spoken!'

(Jesus spoke these words to the two disciples on the road to Emmaus before they recognized him after his resurrection.)

Jesus, I know I can be slow of heart. I understand what you are saying, but I act by reacting. Lately I've been very stressed; there's much on my heart. Jesus, I need to unload or I'll explode. Okay, I'll take a deep breath and tell you what's on my mind. Wow! That's a lot. I cannot possibly accomplish this all. Slow down my racing heart and mind so that I can accomplish only the part that needs to get done. That part is to slow down and pray.

Amen.

Luke 24:32

They asked each other, "Were not our hearts burning within us while we talked with us on the road and opened the Scriptures to us?"

Jesus, after the disciples talked with you, you opened their eyes. You quoted the Scriptures that started in Genesis and continued through Revelations. It's all about you, Jesus. Kindle a fire in my heart, Lord; make it be a light that others can see. I pray that no one or nothing will be a wet blanket to dampen your words ablaze in my heart.

Amen.

Romans 10:9

That if you confess with your mouth, that "Jesus is Lord," and believe in your heart that God raised him from the dead, you will be saved.

Jesus, I know I am saved. I believe this fact, so why am I so troubled? Why all this sadness? Where are you? I feel like Job who lost everything. You tested him, but he was all the stronger for it. In Job 23:10 Job says, "But he knows the way that I take; when he tested me, I will come forth as gold." My prayer is that, like Job, I'll be able to say the same thing because I believe in the depths of my heart I am saved, and will be refined like gold. This is a process. Lord, bear with me.

Amen.

Psalm 24:3–4a

Who may ascend the hill of the Lord? Who may stand in his holy place? He who has clean hands and a pure heart.

Being in health care, it seems like I wash my hands a billion times a day. I do this to take the best care of my patients and my own health, too. Now, what about purifying my heart? That's not easy. I carry hurts from past failures and stuff from present frustrations in my life. Today I ask you, Jesus, to purify my heart. You cleansed me in the water of baptism and you continue to work in my life to this day. Baptize me again. Baptize my heart; make it pure.

Amen.

Psalm 147:3–5

He heals the brokenhearted and binds up their wounds.

He determines the number of the stars and calls them each by name.

Great is our Lord and mighty in power; his understanding has no limit.

Lord, will you help me?	What do you need?
My heart is broken; it needs a Band-Aid.	You have been crying a lot. Why?
I'm sad—someone I love has died.	I know; they are here with me.
I'm jealous of that.	Look up at the stars.
There are so many.	Yes, you can't count them
When I look at the stars, am I seeing heaven?	In your limited way, yes.
I feel so alone.	I understand that, but you aren't.
I love them.	I know. I do, too.
My heart is broken.	I love you, too, you know.
I needed to hear that.	I will say it as many times as there are stars in the sky.
I love you.	I love you.

Amen. (The last thing both of my parents said to me before they passed was, "I love you.")

Psalm 11:2

For look, the wicked bend their bows; they set their arrows against the strings to shoot from the shadows ay the upright in heart.

Today, Lord, I pray for protection. What lurks in the shadows? Who or what is aiming arrows my way? It doesn't matter because I have the armor of God (Ephesians 6:10–19). I have the helmet of salvation, shoes of readiness, breastplate of righteousness, belt of truth, shield of faith, and lastly, the sword of the spirit (Word of God). With all this, Lord, I need not fear, for you've got my back and my heart as well.

Amen.

Psalm 14:1

The fool says in his heart, "There is no God." They are corrupt, their deeds are vile; there is no one who does good.

They say, "There is no God."

I say, "There is so a God."

They say, "It's just luck."

I say, "It's just love."

They say, "God is dead"

I say, "God died for me."

I say, "Jesus loves me; this I know."

I ask you, "What does your heart say?"

Amen.

Psalm 16:7

I will praise the Lord who counsels me; even at night my heart instructs me.

Lord, as I go to sleep tonight, I pray for your counsel to guide me tomorrow, your comfort to get restful sleep, and the courage to get up and face the day ahead.

Amen.

Deuteronomy 8:5

Know then in your heart that as a man disciplines his son, so the Lord your God disciplines you.

God, don't we infuriate you sometimes? Do we just make you cry? I know my children make me feel that way. On the other hand, I love my kids so much. Limits are set, lines are crossed, and consequences happen. After tears, there are hugs. Thank you for being our heavenly parent.

Amen.

Psalm 41:6

Whenever one comes to see me, he speaks falsely, while his heart gathers slander, then he goes out and spreads it abroad.

Holy One, help me not to gossip. It is so easy to get pulled into conversations that slander others. Help me to build up, not tear down, especially when I step on others just to make me look better. I remember the old saying, "If you can't say anything nice, don't say anything at all." Yet I also need to be honest and not hurtful. I need to state my opinion, but not at the expense of others.

Zip my lip, but speak what's true.

Choose a kind voice the whole day through.

Amen.

Proverbs 4:3–4

When I was a boy in my father's house, still tender, and an only child of my mother, he taught me and said, "Lay hold of my words with all your heart; keep my commandments and you will life."

Heavenly Father, today I'd like to just thank you for parents, be they young or experienced ones. Generations have come and gone, yet I'd like to ask my heavenly Father to take care of my family. Bless my family and keep them safe: sisters, brothers, mom, dad, grandparents, great-grandparents, grandchildren, and all adopted folks I may not have mentioned. This prayer is for them all. Bless them, Lord. Hold them safely in your arms, because I wish I were holding them safely in mine.

Amen.

Proverbs 21:1

The king's heart is in the hand of the Lord; he directs it like a watercourse wherever he pleases.

Lord, guide, protect, direct, calm, enrich, energize, establish, ground, motivate, purify, enliven, and humble the hearts of all persons in leadership roles, be they in our country, business, community or church. Establish your kingdom, Lord, in their hearts and hold them safely in your hands.

Amen.

Proverbs 21:2

All a man's ways seem right to him, but the Lord weighs the heart.

Sometimes my heart feels heavy, Lord. Stress, worry, and fear all weigh it down. Life happens, and it is not easy, but you know that. You walked among us, Jesus. You know first-hand what we face.

Take the hurry from my worry.

Press the wrinkles from my stress.

There's nothing to fear; the Lord is near.

He makes my heart feel light.

Amen.

Ecclesiastes 7:21–22

Do not pay attention to every word people say, or you may hear your servant cursing you---for you know in your heart that many times you yourself have cursed others.

Jesus, I am so sensitive to what people say about me. I take everything to heart. That being said, I take things the wrong way. On the other hand, I need to be careful about what I say about others. While you were here on earth, Lord, the Pharisees spoke against you. But what did you do? You never spoke back, even to the point of being wrongly accused, convicted and sentenced to death on the cross. You said nothing. Help me, Jesus, to have a thicker skin, to take criticism, to think before I speak, but to have the guts to speak up when I know in my heart something is wrong or unjustified. Help me to be more like you and to have a brave and sincere heart.

Amen.

Acts 2:46

Every day they continued to meet together in the temple courts. They broke bread in their homes and ate together with glad and sincere hearts.

Jesus, when I invite friends and family into my home, may they encounter graciousness. May my home be a loving place, because you, dear Lord, are the heart of my home, and because your home is in my heart.

Amen.

Deuteronomy 10:12

And now O Israel, what does the Lord your God ask of you but to fear the Lord your God, to walk in all his ways, to love him, to serve the Lord your God with all your heart and with all your soul.

It's pretty clear what you are asking in this passage. We should fear you, serve you, walk in your ways and love you. As I reflect on this passage, I feel more equipped to handle whatever lies ahead. It's like looking at a map before going on a journey. I will walk in your ways today, Lord.

Amen.

Deuteronomy 11:13

So if you faithfully obey the commands I am giving you today---to love the Lord your God and serve him with all your heart and with all your soul.

God, how can I serve you today?

Is it by giving money to a cause?

Is it by organizing a fundraiser?

Is it by going on a mission trip?

Or is it by giving a dollar to that homeless guy I pass every day on my way home?

It's all service.

It's about being involved and getting your hands dirty.

It's about washing the feet of other people,

Like you did, Jesus.

I can do anything you put on my heart to serve you.

What will it be today, Lord?

Amen.

Deuteronomy 15:10

Give generously to him and do so without a grudging heart; then because of this the Lord your God will bless you in all your work and in everything you put your hand to.

God, help me keep my hands open to give and not receive,

And my heart open to stand up for what I believe.

Make me generous, not grudging, in what I do,

Blessing always the work I put my hands to.

Amen.

1 Chronicles 29:17

I know, my God, that you test the heart and are pleased with integrity. All these things have I given willingly and with honest intent. And now I have seen with joy how willingly your people who are here have given to you.

God, test my heart, look inside, really look. What do you see? Honesty, integrity, sincerity, willingness, and joy. Now, Lord, you know I am not perfect, but a work in progress. As long as I'm making strides toward achieving these positive attributes, I'm on the right track. Keep me going in the right direction today and always.

Amen.

2 Chronicles 9:23

All the kings of the earth sought audience with Solomon to hear the wisdom God had put in his heart.

I wish I could have met Solomon. Lord, was he really that smart? I'd say yes, because you, Lord, put the wisdom in his heart. He knew that fact, and then he shared it with people. Lord, I can pray for wisdom, too. Regarding any decision, problem, or joy, Lord, I will be on my knees in prayer before I move forward. Today I will pray for wisdom regarding _____ (fill in your situation).

Amen.

Ezra 7:27

Praise be to the Lord, the God of our fathers, who has put it into the king's heart to bring honor to the house of the Lord in Jerusalem in this way.

Yes, praise God.

I praise you for putting people in leadership positions who follow your ways.

Yes, thank you, Lord.

I thank you for working in and through the hearts of these people to accomplish great things.

Yes, Lord, this way is your way.

Today, I choose to obey; I won't stray or get in the way

Of those whose gifting is leadership.

Amen.

Job 33: 3–4

My words come from an upright heart; my lips will sincerely speak what I know. The Spirit of God has made me; the breath of the Almighty gives me life.

Almighty God,

What do I know?

You created me, Lord; your spirit dwells within me.

But what do I feel? I feel exhausted at present.

With each miraculous breath, my life moves ahead.

Inhale—I pray.

Exhale—today.

Inhale—to perfuse my heart.

Exhale—with peace.

Amen.

Colossians 3:22

Slaves obey your earthly masters in everything; and do it, not only when their eye is on you and to win their favor, but with sincerity of heart and reverence for the Lord.

Lord, to be sincere means to really mean it. No false pretenses, no under lying motive, no hidden agenda. What I do in secret should match what people see me do in plain sight. May I work hard (even when no one is looking) to be sincere and to show respect to all people, including coworkers, family, friends, strangers—everybody.

Amen.

Luke 2:19

But Mary treasured up all these things and pondered them in her heart.

Mary, mother of the Savior, what treasure you carried, what a loss you suffered, and what a faith you had in God's plan. I treasure my children; I worry about them, too. They were once such a part of me, but now they are all grown up. I miss my babies. My children will always be in my heart. I pray for the Lord's protection to surround them; I pray for the Lord to lead them and keep them safe. I will always be their parent, but I know they have a heavenly Father who loves them and treasures them as much as I do. It gives my heart comfort to remember this fact.

Amen.

Exodus 7:3–4

But I will harden Pharaoh's heart, and though I multiply my miraculous signs and wonders in Egypt, he will not listen to you. Then I will lay my hand on Egypt and with mighty acts of judgment I will bring out my divisions, my people the Israelites.

Lord God of Israel, when I read the story of Moses and the escape of the Israelites from captivity in Egypt, I do see your mighty acts. The story, which really happened, gives homage to the God who worked through real people (Moses, the Israelites, Pharaoh, and the Egyptians) to get results. The words that speak to me today are "I multiply" and "my divisions." To me, these are math terminologies.

God, you are infinite, but you work in real time and in real people's lives. God's math turns the ordinary into extraordinary. By dividing the Red Sea, you created an escape plan for the enslaved people of Israel. By providing manna every day for them to eat, you multiplied their chances of survival. And I could go on and on about the plagues. Let's just say, "You are so mighty!" I praise you and thank you, God, for your mighty presence in my life, too.

Amen.

Deuteronomy 11:2–4

Remember today that your children were not the ones who saw and experienced the discipline of the Lord your God: his majesty, his mighty had, his out stretched arm; the signs he performed and the things he did in the heart of Egypt, both to Pharaoh king of Egypt and to his whole country; what he did to the Egyptian army, to his horses and chariots, how he overwhelmed them with the waters of the Red Sea as they were perusing you.

Oh Lord, my God, I have tried to tell others about you. What if they do not seem to listen or even care? Things I experience, namely the healing of illness or the loss of loved ones, may not be exactly what others experience, but they increase my empathy for others. Your mighty hand has been at work all through my life. Whether I see it or not, you, mighty God, have never, ever let me go. You have caught me when I've fallen and rejoiced with me in a job well done. And in all the in-between times, Lord, we meet in the discipline of prayer. I will remember your faithfulness always.

Amen.

1 Kings 3:12

I will do what you have asked. I will give you a wise and discerning heart, so that there will never have been anyone like you, nor will there ever be.

Dear God, discernment is knowing the truth, trusting the signs, and filtering out what is not true. Wisdom is not measured in an I.Q., but in how people use their intelligence, goodness, and fairness in relationship to others. I pray that these words describe my heart.

Amen.

Nehemiah 4:6

So we rebuilt the wall till all of it reached half its height, for the people worked with all their heart.

Today I pray to work hard. I want to be the person who sticks to a job until it's finished. It's funny that this prayer is being written toward the end of this book. I need to stick to it, work hard (even though it's a labor of love, too), and get it done. Keep me going, Lord.

Amen.

Job 10:13

But this is what you concealed in your heart, and I know that this was in your mind.

Great God, what is concealed in my heart today? Joy. I had an amazing surprise. I have so many people I am thankful for, Lord. I love to give people hugs and really mean it. There's joy in my heart, and I show it through appreciating the people who bring this joy into my life. Sometimes days can get tense, yet it is so wonderful being surrounded by people who truly care and whom I trust completely. Another way to share joy is by smiling, Lord. My joy shows in my heart through hugs and smiles. I appreciate all the friends you have put into my life. I will name them as they come into my thoughts.

I do so appreciate all these folks. Thank you for the gift of friendship.

Amen.

Psalm 5:9

Not a word from their mouth can be trusted; their heart is filled with destruction. Their throat is an open grave; with their tongue they speak deceit.

This psalm draws an ugly picture. Destructive words: may they never come from my lips. My heart and mouth are connected; what's inside can come out only if I let it. Be the gatekeeper to my sentences today, Lord.

Amen.

Psalm 14:1

The fool says in his heart, "There is no God." They are corrupt, their deeds are vile; there is no one who does good.

How can you look at a beautiful sunrise or sunset, hear a newborn baby cry, or feel your heart beating in your own chest and say, "There is no God?" You can't. Every heartbeat is God living within, and every breath is God initiated. May I never take this for granted, not even for a moment.

Amen.

Psalm 19:8

The precepts of the Lord are right, giving joy to the heart. The commands of the Lord are radiant, giving light to the eyes.

Lord of light,

I am in the dark, stumbling around without you.

With you as my flashlight and lighthouse,

I can see obstacles and avoid them, or deal with them.

Shed your radiance to illumine my situation.

Help me see what it is that might make me stumble.

Give light to my eyes, while keeping me humble.

Amen.

Psalm 22:14

I am poured out like water, and my bones are out of joint. My heart has turned to wax; it has melted away with in me.

If water doesn't move, it becomes a stagnant puddle. What good is wax that's not put to use as a candle? Bones and muscles need exercise to stay fit. Help me not to be stagnant, Lord. Light a fire within my heart that motivates me to keep moving forward. Keep me going, Lord.

Amen.

Psalm 39:3

My heart grows hot within me, and as I meditate, the fire burned; then I spoke with my tongue ...

Lord, I realize you have a sense of humor because this verse made me smile. I am a middle-aged lady, author, nurse, mother, and wife. I wear many hats, but the "growing hot" reference really hits home with me. I am truly thankful for where I am in my life now, and I appreciate the good and the bad, for both have helped me grow as a person. May the words I speak today express my appreciation of where I am in life. I don't want to be a complainer, Lord. As I mature in my faith, may I realize that I always have things to learn and to teach others. Lord, today I appreciate where I find myself. Use me, especially through the words I speak. May they reflect this appreciation.

Amen.

Psalm 64:6

They plot injustice and say, "We have devised a perfect plan!" Surely the mind and heart of man are cunning.

Here's that mind-heart connection again, Lord. Cunning to me means to be sharp, on your game, up-to-date, with it, smart, savvy. So many days I feel left behind. Trying to keep up with technology takes so much energy. There's an App for everything—"**A P**erfect **P**lan." Hey, that's a God App. How about this one? **A P**eaceful **P**ath, or **A P**ositive **P**erson. Now, those are my kind of apps. Lord, help me to keep up or slow down to keep in step with the **A**lmighty's **P**erfect **P**lan.

Amen.

Psalm 84:2

My soul yearns, even faints, for the courts of the Lord; my heart and my flesh cry out for the living God.

Living God, I have days when I cry out, "Where are you?" But then I look around me. I see the sun rise or set, I feel the warmth of the sun, I see all the colors of the rainbow, and I feel the love of friends, family, and even strangers all around me. My heart is quieted because I am assured of the presence of my living God.

Amen.

Psalm 97:11

Light is shed upon the righteous and joy on the upright in heart.

Jesus,

Illuminate my heart that steadily beats within.

May righteousness be the lamp that lights my way.

The joy in my steps comes literally from my beating heart,

But spiritual joy in my steps comes from you, Lord.

Amen.

Psalm 143:4

So my spirit grows faint with in me; my heart within me is dismayed.

Lord, what do we do when we don't know what to do? Decisions, decisions, decisions. Left or right? Go or wait? Yes or no? What will it be? I guess I'll just sleep on it, Lord. I'll forget about this decision right now. I really can't do anything about it now anyway. Things will look better in the morning; for now, my heart rests within me. I ask you, Lord, for help in quieting my thoughts. My brain races forward at a million miles an hour sometimes, too. Slow my heart. Slow my thoughts. Wait on the Lord.

Amen.

Proverbs 23:15

My son, if your heart is wise, then my heart will be glad.

Lord, gladness does fill my heart today. It's been a long road recently, a very long road, but things are looking up. The experiences (good, bad, or in-between) add the color to the fabric making up our lives. There are happy and sad colors, but, Lord, you weave them together in a quilt of love that warms us when we're cold. Today I pray for wisdom to help me learn from mistakes and add color to the blanket of life.

Amen.

Psalm 62:4

They fully intend to topple him from his lofty place; they take delight in lies. With their mouths they bless, but in their hearts they curse.

Toppling from a lofty place ... a ladder? The corporate ladder? Sometimes it seems like the people in charge really don't know what they are doing. From my vantage point, I am a worker bee. I see the job that needs to be done, and I just need the resources to do it. From their vantage point, they look down and just see a swarm of bees. So I am going to do something that makes me different. I am going to pray for all my bosses, people in authority, and people I answer to. This prayer is for you.

I'll do my best while you lead this flock.

I will follow, but when the ship starts to rock,

Steady the waves, protect me from loss,

Because I'm working for you, but Jesus is my boss.

Amen.

Ezekiel 11:19

I will give them an undivided heart and put a new spirit in them; I will remove from them their heart of stone and give them a heart of flesh.

God gives me an undivided heart.

He takes away my heart of stone.

God gives me a heart of flesh.

What do I do in return?

Simply have a thankful heart.

Amen.

Acts 8:22

Repent of this wickedness and pray to the Lord. Perhaps he will forgive you for having such a thought in your heart.

Lord God in heaven, forgive me.

You know my heart; it's laid out for all to see.

I'm not covering anything up.

Everything is out in the open.

I confess; I come completely clean.

I stand before the throne of God.

He hears my prayer.

He forgives me.

He restores my soul and lightens my spirit because

Jesus carried my sins to the cross.

How can I ever say thank you?

Thank you for loving me so much.

You gave your only Son to die for me.

It all seems too good to be true.

I am a forgiven, washed-clean child of God.

Amen.

Mark 2:8

Immediately Jesus knew in his spirit that this was what they were thinking in their hearts, and he said to them, "Why are you thinking these things?"

Why am I thinking these things? Lord, I don't know. I have control over my thoughts, yet my mind wanders off sometimes. Second Corinthians 10:5 says, "And we take captive every thought to make it obedient to Christ." While riding on my bike, I thought of a little rhyme: "Take all thoughts captive, tie them in a bow, throw them out the window, and away we go!" So that is goofy, but it helps me to visualize taking hold of my thoughts and literally getting rid of the useless and unnecessary ones. I enjoy being creative and letting my mind wander, but, Lord, reign me in when my thoughts are not productive, and bring my thinking into proper focus.

Amen.

Colossians 3:1

Since then, you have been raised with Christ, set your hearts on things above, where Christ is seated at the right hand of God.

Lord, you are in heaven, and I am here. That makes it really hard to set my heart on things above. I feel like I'd be putting it on a shelf out of reach. That's not how I'm supposed to see things, is it? I'm offering up my heart to you, Lord. Take it away from all the distractions of this world and place it among heavenly thoughts. My brain swims in thought, thoughts of every person I should be praying for right now. Stop. I am taking a deep breath, closing my eyes, and just praying for one person that you, Lord, bring to mind: _____.
Thank you, Lord, for this quiet moment with a friend. All is serene. Hear my prayer from heaven; I've set my heart on it.

Amen.

Luke 2:51

Then he went down to Nazareth with them and was obedient to them. But his mother treasured all these things in her heart.

When is your job as a parent done? Never. I'm always worrying, wondering, and hoping my kids are okay and making good decisions. Jesus, you were a baby, toddler, teen, and adult while you were on earth. You had parents who worried about you, too. Mary, I understand your situation, but being the parent of the Son of God? Wow! Words cannot express the responsibility that was bestowed upon you. Today, I pray for families—all sorts of families—for God blesses them and treasures this bond in his heart.

Amen.

Proverbs 3:5

Trust in the Lord with all your heart and lean not on your own understanding; in all your ways acknowledge him, and he will make your paths straight.

Lord,

I acknowledge you.

My understanding is limited;

Your understanding knows no limits.

I dedicate this book to you alone.

I trust you

With my whole heart.

Your path,

Your way,

Today,

Tomorrow,

And

Always.

Amen.

It's 7:32 p.m. on January 15, 2014, and I am finished. I have done my best. I will keep praying for all the people who read this. When you read this and one of the prayers jumps out at you, well, it was written with you in mind. There is a God who is so great and so good, and most importantly, he loves you with all his heart.